Pan Study Aids

Economics

D. P. Baron, J. F. Connor

Pan Books London and Sydney
in association with **Heinemann Educational Books**

First published 1980 by Pan Books Ltd,
Cavaye Place, London SW10 9PG
in association with Heinemann Educational Books Ltd
  5 6 7 8 9
© D. P. Baron and J. F. Connor 1980
ISBN 0 330 26114 2
Printed and bound in Great Britain by
Richard Clay (The Chaucer Press) Ltd, Bungay, Suffolk

PAN STUDY AIDS

Accounts and Book-keeping
Biology
British Government and Politics
Chemistry
Commerce
Economics
Effective Study Skills
English Language
French
Geography 1   *Physical and Human*
Geography 2   *British Isles, Western Europe, North America*
German
History 1   *British*
History 2   *European*
Human Biology
Maths
Physics
Sociology
Spanish

Brodies Notes on English Literature

This long established series published in Pan Study Aids now
contains more than 150 titles. Each volume covers one of the
major works of English literature regularly set for examinations.

Contents

Acknowledgements

The publishers are grateful to the following exam boards, whose addresses are listed on pages 5–6, for permission to reproduce questions from examination papers:

Associated Examining Board, Joint Matriculation Board, University of London Schools Examination Council, Oxford Delegacy of Local Examinations, Royal Society of Arts Examinations Board, Welsh Joint Education Committee.

The exam boards

The addresses given below are those from which copies of syllabuses and past examination papers may be ordered. The abbreviations (AEB, etc) are those used in this book to identify actual questions.

Associated Examining Board,   (AEB)
Wellington House,
Aldershot, Hants GU11 1BQ

University of Cambridge Local Examinations Syndicate,   (CAM)
Syndicate Buildings, 17 Harvey Road,
Cambridge CB1 2EU

Joint Matriculation Board,   (JMB)
(Agent) John Sherratt and Son Ltd,
78 Park Road,
Altrincham, Cheshire WA14 5QQ

University of London Schools Examinations Department,   (LOND)
66–72 Gower Street,
London WC1E 6EE

Northern Ireland Schools Examinations Council,   (NI)
Examinations Office,
Beechill House,
Beechill Road,
Belfast BT8 4RS

Oxford Delegacy of Local Examinations,   (OX)
Ewert Place,
Summertown,
Oxford OX2 7BZ

Oxford and Cambridge Schools Examination Board,   (O & C)
10 Trumpington Street,
Cambridge CB2 1QB

Royal Society of Arts,   (RSA)
18 John Adam Street,
London WC 2

Scottish Certificate of Education Examining Board,   (SCOT)
(Agent) Robert Gibson and Sons, Ltd,
17 Fitzroy Place,
Glasgow G3 7SF

Southern Universities Joint Board,   (SUJB)
Cotham Road,
Bristol BS6 6DD

Welsh Joint Education Committee,   (WEL)
245 Western Avenue,
Cardiff CF5 2YX

1 Guide to revision and examinations

Revision

There is no short cut to examination success. To guarantee a pass, only one piece of advice can be given to students: quite simply, *learn and understand the whole syllabus*. This is especially true for candidates taking examinations that include an objective test paper, because one of the reasons for using this form of examination is to test the whole syllabus and discourage partial coverage and question spotting.

Revision means looking again at something, and in the case of examination revision, this means another look at all the material which has been studied throughout the course. Revision is not a substitute for steady work over a period. It is a way of recalling knowledge and understanding and marshalling information so that it can be presented in a suitable form for examination purposes. Sometimes it helps to have familiar material presented in a different form which is how this study guide can be of use.

The topic-by-topic revision programme suggested in this book could be used in the following way:

1 Choose a topic for revision and read the introductory synopsis and the subject outline in that chapter. This will give a broad, general picture and should help you to recall a deeper treatment of the topic, in your basic textbook or in notes made when you first studied the topic.

2 Approach the topic from the examiner's viewpoint. What are the basic concepts? What is the core of knowledge required? Which aspects of the topic are most suited to questions? Try to do your own thinking, producing your own answers to these questions, before looking at the rest of the chapter.

3 Go back to the subject outline and memorize the material under each sub-heading. There is no alternative to memorizing the core

of each topic. Many candidates enter the examination thinking that common sense, a general understanding of economic principles or regular reading of the financial press will guarantee success. This is most certainly not the case. Marks are awarded for factual content and therefore the basic facts must be learned.

4 After memorizing the core material, select a question, perhaps one answered at the end of the chapter. Jot down the various points you may wish to include and marshal them into some sort of order.

5 Throughout the book you will note words printed in **bold type**. It is important that you should understand and know all these words. Keep a list of these and note their meanings and re-read them regularly until you are confident that you know them.

6 Compare the content of your outline with the content in the chapter. If you have four or five major points then you have adequate knowledge for a pass. The actual grade achieved will depend on additional points made and the extent to which all points are adequately expanded.

7 It is most important to be totally familiar with the definitions of the major economic terms mentioned in each chapter. Most of these will be found in the Glossary at the end of this study guide.

8 Familiarize yourself with the format of the examination paper which you will be taking. Past papers can be very useful as part of revision, giving an indication of the style of question which you may be asked.

9 Practise answering all the types of question you may have to face in the examination within the time allowed, so that you get a good idea of how long an essay should be or how much thinking time can be allowed for objective questions.

Examination technique

Too much emphasis can be placed on examination technique. It is no substitute for steady work over the whole course and sensible revision. It cannot produce a pass for a weak, badly prepared candidate. What it can do is help a good candidate present his or her store of knowledge in a way which best reflects his or her true ability.

The following guidelines may help:

1 Read the instructions at the top of the question paper carefully. Note the total time available, those questions which are compulsory and the number of optional questions which have to be answered. If revision has included familiarization with past papers, all that

will be necessary is to check that there are no
usual instructions.

2 Work out a rough timetable, allocate the available time and on
as you finish each question that you are using the time sensibly.

3 Before attempting a question read it three times and underline
the key words. This may appear to be childish advice, but
experience has shown it to be essential. Thus, with a question
such as '*What is the purpose of calculating the national income?*',
by underlining the word <u>purpose</u>, there is a guarantee that the
candidate will not produce an answer to the question '*How is the
national income calculated?*'.

4 Read the question carefully and decide whether you understand
all parts of it. If you do not understand the point of the question
and it is an optional one, no matter how well you know the topic
leave the question alone. No marks are given for irrelevant
material. Thus, with a question such as '*How can direct and
indirect taxes be used to control inflation?*', there is no point in
listing all the taxes you know and expanding on them in depth
if you cannot relate fiscal policy to controlling inflation.

5 Once you have decided to answer a question, jot down the points
you are going to make. Usually four or five major points are
required for a pass. Discipline yourself to think and plan for five
minutes. Time is not usually a constraining factor in an economics
examination.

6 Allow a separate paragraph for every point. Expand each point
fully, bearing in mind the questions how? and why? If you
allocate separate paragraphs examiners will be able to see clearly
where to give marks and no point you have made will be missed.

7 It is useful to know that no marks are awarded for introductions
and conclusions. Neat writing and well punctuated work facilitate
the award of marks but marks are only awarded for facts, hence
the importance of memory work.

8 Ask yourself if a diagram can usefully be inserted into your
answer. In some questions, such as those dealing with demand
and supply, it is essential. No marks are given for special colouring
or artistic effects – such an approach is simply time wasting.

9 Always attempt the full number of questions required. Many
candidates spoil their chances by answering only three questions
when they are asked to do four. Remember that the first five
marks on any essay question are much easier to obtain than the
last five marks.

Give yourself time to check through your completed paper, looking for simple mistakes – a 'not' missed out which completely changes the meaning of what you meant to say, demand curves labelled as supply curves etc.

Note Bear in mind that the maximum number of marks you can earn in any one essay question is 20. On the 'possible marking schemes' the breakdown of marks often adds up to more than 20, but this is only because examiners want to allow themselves leeway in order to give you as many marks as they can.

Advice on how to approach objective tests and data questions in examinations is given in the next two sections of this chapter.

Objective tests

In recent years objective testing has become a part of many O level examinations in economics. This is because some examiners have had misgivings about relying solely on the traditional 'essay' type examination which tests a candidate's skill in selecting and presenting relevant information. Also marking presents certain problems. However tight a marking schedule is produced, some human judgement is always involved in deciding whether marks have been earned. Where there is a wide choice of questions it is possible for two candidates to answer two completely different sets of questions and the problem of comparability of question difficulty arises. Objective tests do ensure that all candidates are submitted to an identical test, the marking of which is not subject to human error. In other words it is an attempt to be fair to all candidates.

In addition, objective tests can be useful to assess skills which essays do not necessarily demonstrate, for instance numerical skills and some forms of logical reasoning.

A final reason for using objective tests is that it is possible to test over the whole syllabus, whereas essay type examinations must be selective, sometimes favouring the lucky 'question spotter' and penalizing a candidate who may have covered more of the syllabus but has no opportunity to use much of what he has learned.

Types of objective test
There are four types of test which O level candidates are likely to meet.

Multiple choice A question or statement is put in the form of a 'stem' with four or five options from which the candidate has to choose one to complete the statement or answer the question correctly.

Which of the following calculations will determine the balance of trade?
(a) *(visible imports + invisible imports) — (visible exports + invisible exports)*
(b) *(visible imports + visible exports) — (invisible imports + invisible exports)*
(c) *(the balance for official financing) — (the balancing item)*
(d) *(invisible exports) — (invisible imports)*
(e) *(visible exports) — (visible imports)*

The best approach to this type of question, which asks for a recall of a definition or formula, is to start by ignoring the options and attempt to define balance of trade yourself. If your definition coincides with option (e) your problems are over. If you have incorrectly learned the definition and remember it as being (d), there is nothing that can be done at this stage. If you have a vague recollection that the balance of trade is something to do with exports and imports, you can restrict your range of possible guesses by eliminating those alternatives which are obviously wrong. (b) involves adding imports and exports, which does not make much sense. (c) is meant to tempt only those who have not covered the topic at all. You are then left with three possible alternatives and you must decide which one rings the most familiar bell in your mind.

Multiple completion A similar exercise to the multiple choice question, though here the candidate is offered a choice of four or five different combinations of options.

Which of the following measures might a government use to try to reduce cost-push inflation?

1 Increase indirect taxation
2 Remove subsidies on raw materials
3 Impose a wealth tax
4 Limit wage increases through an incomes policy

Answer (a) *if 1 only*
    (b) *if 2 and 3 only*
    (c) *if 3 and 4 only*
    (d) *if 4 only*
    (e) *if none of the above.*

Again the best approach is to attempt to answer the question without looking at the options. Cost-push inflation occurs when prices go up because the costs of manufacture go up. These costs may include labour, raw materials, fuel, transport etc. Any attempt to reduce cost-push inflation must work through reducing these costs or preventing further rises. Look then at the measures suggested (1–4). 1 and 2 will result in increased costs, 3 will have no direct effect on costs, 4 will have some effect on slowing down labour cost increases. Check the options available and you will see that (*d*) offers '4 only' as a possible answer. If you are certain about some of the measures offered but doubtful about others, you may be able to narrow your choice by limiting the possibilities to those which include the ones of which you are certain. For example, if you know that 4 will reduce costs and that 1 and 2 will increase costs, your choice is restricted to (*c*) or (*d*).

Matching pairs Two lists are given and the candidate has to select from one list to match up with items in the other. Sometimes the lists are of equal length and each item must be used; at other times items in one list may be used more than once or not at all.

List 1: place or region	*List 2: description*
1 London	(*a*) *Once dependent on coal and shipbuilding*
2 Aberdeen	(*b*) *New Town*
3 Cornwall	(*c*) *Few large towns and a scattered population*
4 Harlow	(*d*) *Benefiting from North Sea oil*
5 The NE of England	(*e*) *Large consumer market, attracts new industry*

Match List 1 with the best description from List 2 using each description once.

Since all the items in List 2 must be used, the technique for this sort of question is to match up first those items of which you are sure and thus restrict the extent to which guessing is needed.

List 1: financial institutions	*List 2: securities*
1 Discount houses	(*a*) *Treasury bills*
2 Joint stock banks	(*b*) *Mortgages*
3 The Bank of England	(*c*) *Premium bonds*
4 Building societies	(*d*) *Hire purchase advances*

Match the institution in List 1 with the most appropriate security in List 2. Each item in List 2 may be used once, more than once or not at all.

This type of question is more difficult than the first type of matching pairs question because it reduces the extent to which guessing is possible. The best approach is to concentrate on List 2 and use your background information. Hire purchase is dealt with by finance houses; premium bonds are managed by the Post Office; mortgages are given by building societies; Treasury bills are issued by the Treasury through the Bank of England, which then sells them to the discount houses who in turn sell them to joint stock banks. Looking now at List 1, the correct answer becomes *1 (a)*; *2 (a)*; *3 (a)*; and *4 (b)*. *(c)* and *(d)* were put in to distract you.

Assertion/reason questions This is often a difficult type of question, calling for the ability to think clearly and to understand how one statement relates to another. The candidate is asked to consider two statements, the second of which is offered as an explanation of the first. There are five possible alternatives.

1 The first statement is true and the second is a correct explanation of the first.
   Assertion *In a free market the forces of demand and supply determine the price of a commodity.*
   Reason *An excess of demand for the commodity will force the price up until demand falls to equal the available supply.*
2 The first statement is true, and the second statement is also true but is not a correct explanation of the first.
   Assertion *In a free market the forces of demand and supply determine the price of a commodity.*
   Reason *Price elasticity of demand measures the reponsiveness of demand to changes in price.*
3 The first statement is true but the second statement is false.
   Assertion *In a free market the forces of demand and supply determine the price of a commodity.*
   Reason *Demand is equal to supply at all price levels.*
4 The first statement is false but the second statement is true.
   Assertion *In a free market demand and supply are always equal at all prices for all commodities.*
   Reason *Price elasticity of demand measures the responsiveness of demand to changes in price.*
5 The first statement is false and the second statement is also false.
   Assertion *In a free market demand and supply are always equal at all prices for all commodities.*
   Reason *Price elasticity of demand measures the responsiveness of demand to changes in the quantity of supply.*

This type of question calls for a calm unflustered approach. Read each statement slowly, making sure you read what is there and not what you assume it is going to say, e.g. in alternative 5 above the reason starts off as if it is going to be the correct definition of price elasticity of demand and goes wrong only at the end. If the wording of the question is very abstract or general, as in the examples given, try to substitute real examples to get a better understanding. For instance, think about the demand and supply for strawberries and test the statements in that light.

Approach to objective test papers

The usual requirement for O level candidates is to answer about thirty questions in forty-five minutes. For most candidates this is an ample time allowance, but unprepared candidates can panic as the question paper tends to be large and the task seems daunting. It is advisable to look at previous examination papers and the answer sheets provided to familiarize yourself with what is required. A particular type of pencil is usually required (HB). Clear instructions are given, usually on the front of the booklet, about the way in which answers must be given, for example by joining dots or ticking boxes. If you are familiar with the procedure before going into the examination room you may save yourself needless worry.

Because all questions carry equal marks – unless there is some indication to the contrary – there is little point in spending a long time pondering over a single question. The best approach is to start at the beginning and to move through the paper steadily, dealing first with those questions about which you are reasonably certain and do not need to think about. Having been once through the paper in this way, begin again, spending a little more time on those questions which you find more searching. At this stage ignore any questions which you do not understand or know you cannot answer correctly. Use your time sensibly, going through the paper several times, adding a few more answers each time. When the permitted time is nearly up, fill in any blank questions there may be by guessing, narrowing your options as far as possible. Unless clearly stated on the paper, there is no penalty for a wrong answer and therefore you may improve your performance a little by guessing. Try to make sure that you have time to check your answers, especially the easy ones you did first, in order to spot careless mistakes such as ticking (b) when you meant to tick (a).

Many students have strong feelings about objective tests. Some feel frustrated that they are limited in the choice of answers because the answer they would like to give is (a) (if this . . .) or (b) (if that . . .). Although occasionally weak or bad questions do creep into examination papers, usually all questions have been thoroughly tested for accuracy and any possible doubt about the correct answer has probably been caused by misreading the question. The chance to express yourself is available in other parts of the examination.

Some students think objective tests are easy. This is not usually true. They can be very searching and should never be treated lightly.

Practice in tackling all types of objective tests can be not only very helpful examination preparation but also a good way of testing understanding and identifying those parts of the O level syllabus that are your weak spots.

Data response questions

Some examination boards now include a data response question as part of their O level examination in economics. In this kind of testing you would be presented with economic data, in some form, and be expected to be able to interpret it and use it as a basis for further economic analysis.

The object of this kind of question is to find out if you understand economic principles sufficiently well to be able to recognize them in unfamiliar situations. This also makes the study of economics relevant to the real world in which we live and not applicable only to an artificial textbook world, where competition is perfect and all consumers are rational.

There are many forms in which the data may be presented: for instance tables, graphs, pie charts and other pictorial forms, even as a passage of prose, such as a newspaper article.

All data response questions require the same approach. You must get 'behind' the question to identify the appropriate part of economic theory and then apply it. However, each type of data presentation has special features worth looking at.

Tables
In tables data is presented as a set of statistics. Many students are unfamiliar with statistical tables and some practice in a simple approach to such data is probably needed. Remember that data in statistical form is meant to be a short, neat way of presenting information. Ask yourself a few questions. What information is the table capable of giving? The title, if there is one, may tell you, e.g. UK balance of payments 1970–75.

Note that it also tells you the limitations of the data: it will not tell you anything about UK balance of payments in 1969 or in 1976. The column headings are also important and should be defined clearly in your mind, e.g. current balance, balancing item etc. What information *is* the table giving? Many students make the mistake of translating a column of figures back into words without making any attempt at interpretation. For instance,

Money supply (M3):
1973, £29,151m; 1974, £34,342m; 1975 £36,160m.

There is no point in saying 'the money supply in nineteen seventy-three was twenty-nine thousand one hundred and fifty-one million pounds...' The significant information being conveyed by these figures is that the money supply increased by about 17 per cent from 1973 to 1974 and by about 5 per cent from 1974 to 1975. Sometimes, as in this case, you may find it helpful to make a simple calculation from the figures given. With a series of figures to examine, it should be possible to spot those figures which stand out for some reason or to identify trends. Very rarely does a table tell the whole story. Sometimes its purpose is merely to provide an example to illustrate an argument. It is often necessary to have some background knowledge of the area to be able to understand the significance of the figures.

Graphs

The purpose of a graph is to show the changing relationship between two variables. It is important to understand clearly which variables are involved. Often, one of the variables is time, usually measured along the horizontal (bottom) axis. Remember that a graph is a series of points, each one of which has two values, a reading on the horizontal scale and a reading on the vertical scale. An example of a graph might be UK unemployment figures over a series of years, with each year being given one figure.

Although graphs are usually shown as continuous lines, often the only valid data is given at the various plotted points along the line. Sometimes it can be misleading to join up points and apparently create information about the space in between them. For example, if the information about UK unemployment figures was given for five-year rather than yearly intervals, it would not be valid to read off a point between two observations to get the correct unemployment figure for that year.

The most important thing for you to look for in graphs are changes in an apparent pattern. For example there may be a steeper upward movement at one period or an observation which seems out of line with the rest. The task then is to suggest reasons for the change. This may involve drawing upon background information, for example your knowledge about government economic policies in force at different times.

Pie charts and other diagrams

Pie charts show how something is shared out. For example, they might show the countries or regions to which the UK exports. In this case each segment of the chart, usually in the form of a circle, will correspond to the proportion of exports going to each area. The key things to do are to understand what it is that is being divided, what are the categories into which it is being divided and what are the relative sizes of the divisions. Often two pie diagrams on the same topic are given and you will be expected to note any significant differences and then to offer some explanation for them.

Histograms and bar charts are ways of presenting information when attention needs to be drawn to several variables at once. The important things to look for are changes in relative size. Again, some explanation may then be needed.

Continuous prose passages

Students who do not like graphs and figures sometimes think that this type of data response question is much easier. It can be deceptive, especially if it is from a newspaper article written in a very chatty style. Never forget that such a question, in this context, is part of an economics examination and therefore your interpretation of it must be against the background of your studies in economics. Establish first what the passage is about and what section of an economics syllabus it relates to. It may be about collecting wastepaper, but at the same time illustrate supply and demand analysis and the determination of price. It may discuss 'perks' for top executives, but it should prompt you to discuss mobility of labour and enterprise or even cost-push inflation.

Sometimes, with this type of data response question, as with all types, you may be asked a series of short questions, which will lead you from one step of understanding and analysis to another. In other cases, you may be asked apparently broad but simple questions such as 'Comment on the data given.' In all cases try to relate your answer to the time allowed. If thirty minutes are given for two questions then obviously one-sentence answers are not appropriate. Similarly if ten questions are asked, in the same time limit, then a two-page answer to one question is not what is wanted.

Our first example of a data response question comes from *Data*

Response Questions in O level Economics.

Changes in weekly and monthly pay (UK averages) (1971 = 100)

	Average money earnings (paid weekly)	Average real earnings	Average money salaries (paid monthly)	Average real salaries
1971	100	100	100	100
1972	112	105	112	105
1973	130	110	126	107
1974	150	112	140	104
1975	200	114	190	109

1 *Plot the data shown in the above table as a series of graphs on the same chart.*
2 *Explain what is meant by 1971=100.*
3 *Which series of figures shows the steepest rate of growth?*
4 *Account for the differences between 'real' earnings/salaries and 'money' earnings/salaries.*
5 *What explanations can you offer for the different rates of change for weekly earnings and monthly salaries?*
6 *What are the limitations to using this type of data for wage negotiations?*

Before answering the specific questions, establish what the table is all about. There are two sets of contrasted pairs: 'money/real' and 'weekly earnings/monthly salaries'. The distinction between 'money' and 'real' is to do with the purchasing power of income and is affected by inflation. The distinction between 'weekly earnings' and 'monthly salaries' is sometimes blurred but broadly contrasts income for manual workers to that of non-manual workers, including managers. In the period 1971–5 there was rapidly rising inflation and efforts were made by governments of both major parties to deal with it, partly by incomes policies. The fact that the figure for 1971, in all columns, is 100, suggests that all the data is in the form of index numbers.

1 When the data is plotted the information from the table comes out in a striking fashion. Money earnings/salaries rise very steeply compared with real earnings/salaries. The upward trend for all variables is broken by the 1974 figure for real salaries.
2 A simple account of index number theory is called for. All data is related on a percentage basis to 1971 figures. Thus in 1975 money earnings were twice as high as in 1971 but in real terms (i.e. what they could buy) they had increased only 14 per cent.

3 The steepest rise is for average money earnings. The easiest way to do this question is to plot the figures and look at the graph that results. This question is intended to check the accuracy of your graph and to see if you can make a simple interpretation from it.

4 The difference is due solely to inflation, i.e. increases in the general price level. If prices remained the same then a 10 per cent increase in money wages would mean a 10 per cent increase in spending power, i.e. real wages.

Note These figures of earnings and salaries are gross, i.e. they do not take into account income tax and other deductions. We are not given figures for disposable income, in real or money terms.

5 It is not possible from the data given, nor even by drawing on background information, to give a definite explanation for the different rates of change for weekly earnings and salaries. All that can be done is to show an awareness of some points which might be relevant. Such points might include the importance of non-monetary benefits, especially to managers; the relative bargaining strengths of manual and non-manual groups of workers; the composition of the sample from which presumably the data was drawn, e.g. some high paid non-manual workers were refused pay increases by the terms of some incomes policies; the government's attitude towards public sector workers.

6 The table deals in UK averages whereas wage negotiations are carried out by sectional groups of workers, each group having special circumstances. The figures might be used as a yardstick for making wage claims but the final offer agreed to will have to take into account the amount of money available for increases, the effects on costs and sales, the effect on employment levels and maybe the attitude of the government towards pay increases.

Our second example of a data response question uses the following table which refers to the structure of employment in Britain.

Distribution of the total workforce (%)

	1901	1979
Primary sector	15	3
Secondary sector	44	36
Tertiary sector	41	61

1 Describe in your own words the information expressed in the above table.
2 What are the main reasons that help explain the trends?

1 The table on p. 19 refers to the changing distribution of the workforce between the primary, secondary and tertiary sectors of the economy between 1901 and 1979. The percentage of the total workforce employed in the primary sector has fallen by 12 per cent to 3 per cent of the current total workforce. The percentage of the workforce engaged in the secondary sector has fallen 8 per cent to a figure of 36 per cent. In contrast the percentage of the workforce engaged in the tertiary sector has increased by 20 per cent to a figure of 61 per cent.

This answer would obtain maximum marks because the following basic rules have been followed.

(a) It is clearly stated what the table is referring to.
(b) A clear reference is made to the *percentage* of workforce employed and *not* the numbers employed. (It is possible for the percentage to drop but the numbers to increase if the size of the workforce has increased, or the opposite.) The table title has been carefully read and understood.
(c) *All* the information is reproduced. It is so obvious that many candidates, though appreciating the trends, regard it as too simplistic to reproduce in words, and consequently they lose marks.

2 The decline in the percentage of the workforce engaged in the primary industries is mainly because of increased mechanization. Thus, a combine harvester or a modern drill in a mine can do the same amount of work in an hour as tens of workers. There are other factors involved. Thus, many natural resources have become exhausted or less productive, for example, in the fishing industry. Additionally, especially in the present employment situation, there has been a drift away from certain occupations, for example, agriculture.

The decline in the secondary sector is almost completely explained by the widespread adoption of labour-saving machinery, partly a result of higher labour costs but also in the search for higher productivity.

The tertiary sector has, as in all advanced economies, become more important. A higher standard of living results in an increased demand for personal services ranging from travel agencies to take-away restaurants to dog boutiques. Hence, the shift of labour to satisfy the demand. The state has become more involved in citizens' well-being, hence the growth of social workers and welfare visitors and so forth. Moreover, the modern complex commercial and economic world demands increased specialists in areas such as advertising, banking and insurance. All have served to increase the percentage of the workforce employed in the tertiary sector.

Again this answer would obtain very high marks; simply because the basic rules have been followed.

(a) This part of the question relies on acquired knowledge.
(b) Each trend is discussed in turn.
(c) The reason for each trend is carefully, perhaps pedantically, spelt out. *But* the examiner has a list of points he is looking for. He can only award marks when you mention these points. So mention them.

Occasionally the two questions are linked together: for example *'Describe and comment on the above table.'* This is asking for exactly the same material. It would assist the examiner (and therefore you) in allocating the marks if you adopted the same approach as in the two-part question. Comment, in other words, means account for or explain.

Our third example illustrates the use of a line graph.

The figure below refers to the average number of hours worked per week.

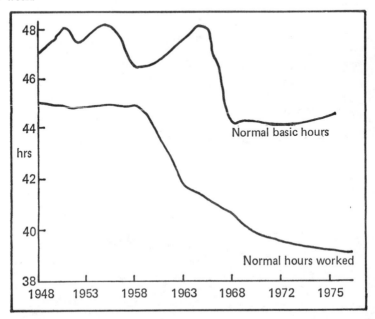

1 Describe the trends in the graphs.
2 What are the main factors that help explain the trends?

1 The two graphs relate to the average hours worked and the changes
in these hours between 1948 and 1975. The working week is shown
at two levels: the basic working week, that is, the minimum number
of hours workers were required to perform and the actual hours
worked which is overtime work added to the minimum working
week. The 'normal' working week has fallen from 45 hours to
$39\frac{1}{2}$ hours a week in this period. The hours of the normal week
remained fairly constant between 1948 and 1960, but fell sharply
between 1960 and 1963 from an average of $43\frac{1}{2}$ to $41\frac{1}{2}$ hours.
Since then there has been a steady decline in the normal working
week to its present level. The actual hours work fluctuated between
45 and 48 hours. The highest level was reached in 1954 with
$48\frac{1}{2}$ hours worked in the average working week. The lowest is
the period 1968–72 with an average of $44\frac{1}{2}$ hours.

The 'normal' working week has fallen more significantly than the
average of the actual hours worked. In consequence the gap
between the two has widened from 2 hours in 1948 to 5 hours in
1975.

Points to note
(a) What the two graphs represent and what years are represented is
clearly stated.
(b) There is a description of the main movement of each graph,
mentioning the initial and final figures – emphasis on any marked
movements.
(c) Reference is made to the widening gap.
All these may seem very obvious *but* to obtain the marks *all* must
be expressed in words.

2 The decline in the minimum working week reflects an increase in
the standard of living. At a certain date, in Britain's case in the
early 1960s, workers through their unions began to demand a
reduction in the working week instead of, or in addition to, wage
increases. This is more pronounced when the government has
imposed a wage freeze or maximum wage norm, which limits
increases and forces negotiators to improve conditions. Increased
mechanization and automation have assisted this process because
output can often be maintained with fewer hours worked. By
successfully reducing the minimum working week unions have made

it necessary in many cases for firms to offer more overtime, if production levels are to be maintained, and thus workers are able to earn overtime bonuses for working what was previously the standard minimum number of hours, hence the increasing divergence between the two graphs. The fluctuation in the average working week is a consequence of the level of economic activity. A period of depression, or falling demand, is reflected in the offer of less overtime work by firms and the converse in times of economic boom.

Note This in effect is a supplementary question. The knowledge required from the answer is not to be found on the graph. Background information is required, knowledge acquired from textbooks. In addition economic reasoning is necessitated. Often answers can be found by simply making deductions and logical conclusions. Thus, for example, the reference to the fluctuations in overtime work is in effect a simple deduction expressed in economic terms.

Occasionally the description and explanation might be asked for by the same question: '*Explain the trends* . . .' The same material would need to be presented in the same manner.

2 The economic problem and economic systems

Synopsis The basic economic problem is that because human wants always exceed resources there is always **scarcity** and choices must be made to decide which **wants** to satisfy and which to leave unsatisfied. There are three broad alternative economic systems which use different approaches to find the best solution to the problem: the **capitalist**, the **collective** and the **mixed economy**. Because the problem cannot be completely solved, each system has advantages and disadvantages.

*

Human wants are unlimited. A teenager is unable to satisfy all his wants for clothes, holidays and leisure activities. A householder is unable to satisfy all his wants for new carpets, furniture and hi-fi equipment. A government is unable to satisfy all the demands of its supporters to provide houses, educational facilities and health facilities.

The wants of individuals remain unfulfilled through a lack of money. For the community as a whole, lack of money is not the cause. A government could easily triple or quadruple the amount of money in circulation without solving all its problems. The reason wants are not satisfied is because there is a lack of resources, called **factors of production.**

To produce any article, to grow any crop or to provide any service, requires a combination of **factor resources**, namely **labour, capital, land** and **enterprise**. For example, drilling for oil in the North Sea requires considerable finance and machinery (capital), a whole range of professional and manual workers (labour), considerable organization (enterprise), as well as the natural resource of oil (land). The problem is that all these factors are in limited supply.

A community has **limited** or **finite** resources to satisfy **unlimited** or **infinite** wants. All wants cannot be met because there is this problem of **scarcity**. This is usually called the **basic economic problem**. The problem is how to allocate limited resources to meet the demands of unlimited wants.

The problem of resource allocation may be defined by asking a series of questions:

1 What commodity or service to make? Implicit in this question is another one: what not to produce? This gives an economic concept known as **opportunity cost**: if the factors of production are available to build either a factory or a school and it is decided to build the factory, then the **real cost** of the factory is the non-building of the school. This real cost is known as opportunity cost.
2 How much of the commodity to produce?
3 How to organize the production of the commodity?
4 How should the proceeds of this production then be distributed?

The way in which these basic decisions are made depends on the way in which a community or country organizes its economic life, i.e. the type of **economy** a country possesses.

In broad terms, three types of national economies have developed in the world:

1 **Capitalist or free enterprise economy,** where all the decisions are made by individuals either as **consumers** or by businessmen as **producers**
2 **Collective or planned economy,** where the decisions are made completely by the state, i.e. the government.
3 **Mixed economy,** where some decisions are made by the state and some by the individual. In reality, most economies are of this type, although the USA approaches the extreme of the capitalist system and China and the USSR approach the extreme of the collective system.

No system is perfect. Perhaps the increasing tendency towards mixed economies suggests that countries are trying to achieve the advantages and benefits of both capitalist and collective approach without the serious disadvantages each system possesses.

The capitalist or free enterprise system

An economy in which individual consumers and businessmen make all economic decisions, without any state interference.

Advantages

1 Firms compete against each other. The result is lower prices, better quality and improved service.
2 A businessman is encouraged to develop new products and more efficient methods of production, because any extra profit is for him. This incentive results in new products and better production.
3 The allocation of the scarce factors of production is determined by the price mechanism. (This is discussed later. See Chapter 10.) This ensures the most efficient use of scarce resources.
4 Individuals are free to buy or sell any products, free to work in any occupation, and free to enjoy a variety of goods.
5 The number of state officials and civil servants is reduced to a minimum. This increases the number available for more productive work and reduces the number of decisions made by people with no business experience.

Disadvantages

1 Monopolies may replace competition and result in exploitation of the consumer. The result may be higher prices, poorer service and no innovation.
2 There may be insufficient investment in new machinery and plant. Profits may not be ploughed back. Industries may be inefficient and outdated.
3 Because profit becomes the object of business:
   (a) luxury items, carrying a high profit margin, will be produced before essential goods and services, which may earn little or no profits.
   (b) unprofitable services, such as education, minor roads, police forces and fire protection, will not be provided.
4 Inequalities of wealth result. In simple terms, the employers become wealthier as profits are made, employees fall behind. Extremes of wealth are always found in capitalist states.
5 The social costs of capitalism are excessive because of the absence of any government interference. Examples of social costs include pollution, slag heaps, traffic congestion and poor planning and siting of factories.
6 Absence of government control and regulation creates a situation in which consumers may be exploited, for example in the areas of quality, safety, pricing and misleading advertisements.

7 There may be wasted resources, e.g. competitive advertising.

The following is an example of the kind of question you might face about free market economies.

1 What are the distinguishing features of a free market economy? What weaknesses of such an economy lead governments to intervene? (AEB)

Collective system

A system where all economic decisions are made by the state.

Advantages
1 The state is able to distribute the wealth of the country equally and fairly amongst all members of the community, removing extremes of poverty and riches.
2 The state is able to ensure that the limited factors of production are utilized in the production of essential goods for the benefit of the majority rather than the production of luxury goods for the minority.
3 The state ensures that there is adequate investment in essential industries, thus guaranteeing a modern efficient industrial structure which will be competitive in world markets.
4 A number of services are, by their very nature, unprofitable, e.g. fire protection, education, maintenance of roads. Unless they are provided by the state there is a danger of inadequate provision.
5 Some services are unsuitable for competition, e.g. gas, electricity and water. These are natural monopolies and therefore best controlled by the state.
6 The state will be concerned about wasteful use, or non-use, of resources, especially human resources. Unemployment will be kept as low as possible.

Disadvantages
1 There is a basic loss of freedom. Workers might be compelled to work in certain industries. There will be a limited range of goods available, because what is produced will be determined by the state.
2 There will be a lack of incentive and innovation. No personal gain will result from increased production or improved efficiency, because all profits go to the state. Therefore there will be few new products or new methods of production.
3 Although some state officials are essential to production, a complete state system usually results in an excessive number of civil servants

carrying out unnecessary jobs and helping to stifle initiative by applying regulations very strictly.
4 Decisions are made initially for the economy as a whole, rather than for small parts of it. If mistakes are made the results can be far reaching. For example the decision on how many acres of potatoes is made centrally instead of thousands of small decisions made by individual farmers.

You might get a question asking you to compare the capitalist system with the collectivist system.

2 What are the advantages and disadvantages of a market economy compared with a command economy? (WEL)

Mixed economy

This is an economy in which decisions are made partly by the state and partly by individuals. The state controls the broad economic framework of the economy, but allows private enterprise to exist within that framework. The aim is to secure the advantages of capitalism and collectivism without their disadvantages.

In the UK the state attempts to control and regulate the broad economic framework in a variety of ways: (at this stage it is sufficient to list government controls, details will be found in later chapters).

1 Nationalization
2 Employment policies
3 Monetary policies, control of inflation/deflation
4 Wage policies
5 Fiscal policies
6 Social welfare policies
7 Balance of payments equilibrium policies
8 Consumer protection
9 Industrial reorganization and regeneration
10 State subsidies

The UK is one of the best examples of a mixed economy, but it must be emphasized that all economies are, to a lesser or greater extent, mixed economies.

3 *What do you consider to be the advantages of a mixed economy in which both private and public sectors exist?* (JMB)

Examination preparation

Objective test study material

To be prepared for objective questions covering this part of the syllabus you should be sure you know the definitions for:
Wants   Factor resources   Factors of production   Land   Labour
Capital   Enterprise   Opportunity cost   Real cost   Collectivism
Capitalism   Mixed economy

Essay questions

There is a wide variety of questions which can be asked on the essay paper calling for a knowledge of the basic economic problem and the types of economic systems that have developed to solve the problem of limited factor resources. Questions vary from the basic, direct question – for example *'What do you understand by the term "mixed economy"?'* or *'What advantages does such a system offer?'* – to the more subtle 'disguised' question such as *'What are the functions of the price mechanism? Comment on its effectiveness.'*

This last question involves a knowledge of supply and demand curves and the concept of equilibrium, a topic which will be discussed in a later chapter. This demonstrates an important point. Economics is a circular subject. Topics are often interdependent and inter-related and cannot be studied in complete isolation.

All answers on the topic of the 'basic economic problem' must, by way of introduction, include the following two paragraphs.

1 A paragraph on scarce resources and unlimited wants. Make full reference to the factors of production.
2 A full discussion of the economic problem and the economic systems which have been developed to solve the problem.

For instance consider the following question:

The basis of the private enterprise economy is the price mechanism. Discuss the relative merits and demerits of this type of economic system.

Para 1 Expand on the idea that all economic systems strive to answer the basic economic problems.
Para 2 Mention that the private enterprise system seeks to answer the problem by the operation of a free market, that resources are allocated

by price and price is determined by the interaction of supply and demand. Use an example or perhaps draw a diagram to show equilibrium and disequilibrium.

Para 3 You could say that this system affords economic advantages. Argue that resources are distributed most efficiently because they are paid exactly what they are worth. Over-production and under-production of a commodity are continuously adjusted.

Para 4 Elaborate upon other advantages such as the gains that follow when personal incentives are rewarded and competition among firms exists. Explain these gains, showing how they develop.

Para 5 Here you could point out that in practice the system of free or private enterprise has disadvantages. The most frequently voiced is the inequality of wealth which results. Explain why and what effects this may have on the economy.

Para 6 Point out that where the consumer is sovereign and profit the motive there is no guarantee of an investment programme. The effects of this would be enormous; for instance resources might be wasted.

Para 7 Or a monopoly situation might develop. Explain why and the possible disadvantages of this. Explain why even where there is an absence of monopoly there is the danger of consumer exploitation.

Para 8 Explain that since profit is the aim of industry, major services, perhaps by their nature less profit making or even non-profit making, will be neglected – education and health for instance. Explain why social costs are heavy.

Obviously all the points cannot be introduced and discussed. Aim to include an explanation of the price mechanism and a balanced approach to advantages and disadvantages.

Possible marking scheme

A detailed mark scheme is impossible: perhaps 8 marks for paragraphs 1 and 2, then up to a maximum of 3 marks for each point developed in the second part of question.

3 Organization of economic activity

Synopsis In order to study economic activity in the UK today it is helpful to use a system of classification, dividing the economy into the public and private sectors. It is then possible to look at the various forms of organizations within each sector, to examine the reasons for each form and its advantages and disadvantages.

*

The production and distribution of goods and the provision of services are carried out by a variety of business enterprises. These differ in size and organization. These enterprises are found in the public sector and private sector.

Public sector That part of the economy run by the state.
Private sector That part of the economy owned and controlled by individuals or groups of individuals.

Public sector

The enterprises in the public sector can be administered in many different ways:

(a) by local authorities, e.g. Manchester Airport.
(b) by bodies created by Parliament, e.g. regional water boards.
(c) by government departments (Ministries), e.g. education, health.
(d) by public corporations. This is the most important form and applies to gas, electricity, coal, air transport, post, iron and steel etc.
(e) indirectly by holding a majority of shares in a firm in the private sector, e.g. British Leyland.

Reasons for having a public sector

1 Some services are natural monopolies and control by the state ensures that the consumer is not exploited, e.g. electricity.
2 Adequate capital is available in high cost industries, e.g. atomic power.
3 Unnecessary duplication and wasteful competition is avoided.
4 Economics of scale may result from production in large units.
5 Non-profitable but socially necessary services are provided, e.g. education and police.
6 The life of declining industries, e.g. steel, may be prolonged to lessen the effects of unemployment.
7 It may be easier to carry out government economic strategy, for instance wage and price policies.
8 Industries which are economically and strategically important may be maintained, e.g. Rolls-Royce.

There are also political reasons which are not relevant here.

Reasons against having a public sector

1 Lack of competition may destroy initiative and create inefficiency.
2 Management is often inexperienced and too readily succumbs to political pressures, e.g. pricing policy and redundancy programmes.
3 Units may be too large, resulting in diseconomies of scale.
4 The public has little control and is rarely consulted, e.g. recent increases in postal charges.
5 Lack of profit motive may result in decreased efficiency.

An essay question about this material may take the following form:
1 What is meant by the public sector? Why is it considered necessary to to have a public sector? (AEB)

Public corporations

Public corporations are bodies created by Parliament to administer nationalized industries. They have the following characteristics:

1 Their organization and structure are laid down by Parliament.
2 Their day-to-day administration is in the hands of a Board appointed by and responsible to the appropriate Minister.
3 The Minister is responsible to Parliament for the efficient running of the industry.
4 They are financed by the Treasury rather than directly by public sources.
5 They are not required to make a profit but simply to balance their

books over a period of time.
6 They are usually **monopolies** (i.e. sole producers of a good or service), for example British Rail and British Gas. There are, however, a few exceptions, e.g. British Airways.
7 Consumer councils are connected with public corporations to facilitate complaints etc.

Private sector

There are several forms that firms in the private sector can take.

Sole proprietor
This is common in farming, retailing and personal services, e.g. window cleaning, hairdressing. In a sole proprietorship a single person owns and controls the business, takes the risks and enjoys the profits.

Advantages of sole proprietorships
1 Because of the incentive afforded, efficiency increases.
2 Rapid decisions can be made; this allows for flexibility.
3 Relationships with workers are usually good so there is less strike action.
4 Good relationships with customers – customer goodwill – is usual.
5 They are easily and cheaply established.

Disadvantages of sole proprietorships
1 Unlimited liability.
2 Illness and holidays can cause problems for the continuous running of the business.
3 Limited finance creates problems:
    (a) It is difficult to expand.
    (b) Recession will affect sole proprietors particularly badly; for instance, unpaid contracts will cause liquidity problems.
4 Ideas and abilities are limited.

Sources of finance for sole proprietors
1 Personal sources, e.g. savings, relatives.
2 Bank loans and overdrafts.
3 Finance houses, e.g. hire purchase.
4 Invoice discounting.
5 Trade credit.
6 Plough back profits.
7 Mortgage property.
8 Government grants, especially in development areas.

Partnerships

In a partnership between two and twenty partners own and control the firm. Exceptions to these restrictions are found in the case of solicitors and accounting firms.

Deed of partnership is a legal requirement stating the status of partners regarding profit sharing, dissolution, etc.

Advantages of partnerships

1 Easily and cheaply created.
2 More capital than sole proprietor.
3 Administrative costs reduced – doctors' surgeries for example.
4 Partners able to specialize – solicitors for example.
5 Management functions shared.
6 More ideas.
7 Good employee and customer relations still exist.

Disadvantages of partnerships

1 Capital is still limited.
2 Decision making is less flexible.
3 Unlimited liability.
4 Personal differences can cause problems in running the business.
5 Dissolution creates problems, especially dissolution caused by the. death of a partner.

Sources of finance for partnerships are similar to those for sole proprietors.

Joint stock companies

The distinguishing feature of joint stock companies is that they have a separate legal existence from those that contribute their capital. The company can sue and be sued as a separate entity.

Public joint stock company

This is the most important form of private enterprise organization. In this category are the major firms in the UK today – Shell, Unilever, ICI, Imperial Tobacco Company.

Advantages of public joint stock companies

1 They are able to attract larger amounts of capital more easily because of the service provided by the **Stock Exchange.**
2 They enjoy limited liability.
3 Shareholders are able to sell their shares.
4 The firm has continuity. Its existence is unaffected by deaths etc.
5 Economies of scale are possible.

Disadvantages of public joint stock companies

1 A minority of shareholders often dominate.
2 Diseconomies of scale can often result.
3 There can be less harmonious relationships with both employees and customer.
4 There is less self-interest, thus less efficiency.
5 Establishing a public joint stock company is an expensive process.

Sources of capital for public joint stock companies

1 Public issue of shares. There are many kinds of shares, e.g.
   (a) **preference shares** These have the first claim on profits but usually receive a low dividend and usually have no voting rights. The dividend on preference shares is fixed.
   (b) **ordinary shares** These do have voting rights. The dividend paid on them fluctuates.
   (c) **deferred shares** Their holders are the last to be paid. The benefit is a higher dividend and proportionally more voting rights.

Shares are advertised by means of a prospectus. The price paid at time of issue is known as the **nominal value** of a share. The share however has a **market value** on the Stock Exchange which could be above or below the nominal value, depending on the current profitability of the firm.

2 Debentures These are loans to a firm at a fixed rate of interest which is paid regardless of the firm's profitability. Thus, the interest is usually low. There are no voting rights for debenture holders.
   A **secured debenture** is a loan guaranteed by the firm's collateral.
3 Plough back profits.
4 Bank loans and overdrafts.
5 HP and leasing.
6 Invoice discounting.
7 Trade credit.
8 Government grants.
9 Industrial and Commercial Finance Corporation, National Enterprise Board and similar specialist financial institutions.

2 Describe the ways by which firms raise capital. (ox)

Organization of public companies

1 Shareholders at annual general meeting elect board of directors.
2 Board of directors elect managing director.
3 Board determine the broad policy of the company. The managing director has responsibility for implementing policy.

4 Rarely do more than a handful of shareholders influence the policy of the firm because
  (a) shareholders are too numerous to act in concert
  (b) shareholders lack management experience
  (c) shareholders usually have shares, and therefore interest, in many firms.

3 Compare joint stock companies with nationalized industries as forms of business organization. (LOND)

Private joint stock companies
Private joint stock companies differ from public companies in that the number of shareholders is limited to fifty; they can only be sold with the consent of all the shareholders; and they cannot obtain capital by selling shares to the general public. Usually these are one-man or family businesses which have been made into a company to gain the advantages of limited liability. As a result, this is the most common form of organization. Currently there are 360,000 private joint stock companies in the UK.

Over 90 per cent of firms are either private companies or sole proprietorships. These survive in competition with the larger public companies for a number of reasons:

1 They provide specialist goods for which there is a small demand, e.g. clothes, furniture.
2 High transport costs can limit the size of the market; for instance, large firms are unable to dominate the bricks market.
3 The size of the market may be limited by the perishable nature of the product, e.g. bread.
4 They may provide personal services, e.g. hairdressing, estate agents, travel agents.
5 The small firm may be able to achieve optimum output at low levels of production, e.g. fashion shoes.
6 A flexible production pattern is possible to respond to changes in demand, e.g. clothes.
7 They are able to concentrate on one product, e.g. brake linings.
8 Product differentiation is used to create brand loyalty, e.g. Cussons soap.
9 They are able to reap external economies and thus reduce costs.
10 Small firms co-operate, e.g. pottery firms engage in joint research.

Co-operatives
In other countries these are found in production. For instance, there are farmers' co-operatives in Denmark and Ireland. But in Britain co-operatives are almost exclusively in retailing.

Producers' co-operative In a producers' co-operative workers establish their own productive units, raise their own capital, elect management from their own ranks and share the profits.

Retail co-operatives
The retail co-operatives have the following characteristics:
1 Capital contributed by members
2 Shares bought by each member limited to £1000 nominal value
3 Shares not sold on Stock Exchange but sold back to co-operative
4 Number of shares unlimited
5 Fixed interest on the shares
6 Surplus profit distributed by a dividend or stamps in an amount proportional to purchases
7 Annual general meeting elects part-time management committee to run society and determine broad policy
8 Management committee appoint full-time staff to implement policy

Co-operative Wholesale Society Retail societies subscribed capital to form CWS. The societies share profits in proportion to their purchases. In the control of the wholesale society, votes by retail societies are in proportion to their purchases.

CWS buys in bulk on behalf of retail societies. This allows them to charge lower prices. It also manufactures own-label products – tea, soap, beans etc. Moreover it has now expanded into banking, insurance, travel and funeral directors.

Advantages of co-operatives
1 Limited liability.
2 As friendly societies, they pay a lower rate of tax on profits.
3 Customers enjoy profits.
4 Economies of scale as a result of buying from CWS.

Disadvantages of co-operatives
1 Minority, often inexperienced in business, monopolize management committee.
2 Because of the method of appointment, and perhaps the low wages, they have difficulty in attracting top businessmen.
3 Some societies are too small to be effective.

You may be faced with a very broad question about the forms of business organization.

4 *What are the main types of business organization found in Britain today?* (ox)

Examination preparation

Objective test study material

Prepare definitions for the following
Public sector Private sector Public company Limited liability Types of shares Debentures Public corporation Co-operative societies Joint stock company

Essay questions
State the main differences between public and private enterprises.
What reasons have been given for the creation of public enterprise in the UK?

Para 1 First you should define the public and private sectors and give examples to illustrate your answer.
Para 2 Contrast ownership by the state to that by individuals.
Para 3 Discuss the different methods of control and management.
Para 4 Discuss the alternative sources of finance: Treasury, Stock Exchange etc.
Para 5 Point out the different market structures – i.e. monopoly versus competition – in which each operates.
  The second part of the question can really be interpreted as an 'old' type question on the reasons for nationalization. Perhaps four or five points are looked for by examiners. Usually one mark is awarded for each point mentioned, an additional mark or marks for development. The usual points made are:

1 Danger of natural monopolies in private hands
2 Maintaining levels of employment
3 Ensuring high levels of investment
4 Economic planning
5 Avoidance of duplication
6 Economies of scale
7 Strategic arguments
8 Political arguments

Possible marking scheme
In the first part of this question, paragraph 1 would be worth 4 marks

while paragraphs 2–5 would be worth 2 marks each to a maximum of 6 marks. Thus, 10 marks in total could be earned in the first part.

In the second part of the question although perhaps four points developed will earn the maximum 10 marks, a list of seven or eight points not developed will usually only obtain half the allocated marks. It is important in essays to develop each point. Unless this is done, marks will be lost.

Examination practice

5 *Examine the main features of*
   (*a*) *sole proprietor*
   (*b*) *partnership.*
   In which areas of industry are they likely to be found? (WEL)
6 *What are the main ways in which private enterprise may raise capital?* (WEL)
7 (*a*) *Outline the main characteristics of a public company.*
   (*b*) *Discuss the advantages of public companies as a form of business organization.* (RSA)
8 *Describe the main sources of finance for each of the following:*
   (*a*) *sole trader or proprietor*
   (*b*) *public company*
   (*c*) *public corporation* (RSA)

4 Population

Synopsis The human part of a nation's resources and, indirectly, all its wants are determined by its population. It is necessary to define and measure the factors which bring about population change because changes in its size and distribution have important economic effects.

*

Population is an important area of study in economics because people are both producers and consumers. The possible answers to the basic economic questions for each economy, 'what shall be produced and for whom?', are affected by the size and nature of the population.

In this chapter the emphasis will be on people as consumers.

Optimum population

Optimum population is an important concept. It relates the size of the population to the standard of living of a country. A country with the ideal size of population, i.e. optimum, in relation to its other resources, will experience a fall in its standard of living if the population increases or decreases. In practice it is never possible to measure precisely the optimum population of any country, because even if accurate data were available, circumstances such as the level of technology and the availability of resources are constantly changing and therefore altering the optimum figure. However, by considering the 'optimum population' in the most general sense, it is possible to relate to situations which do exist, namely 'underpopulation' and 'overpopulation'.

Changes in population

It is impossible to write in general terms about the economic effects of changes in the population. The effects will vary depending on (a) the size of the population, in relation to the optimum, before the change and (b) the reason for the change. Examples of reasons are a decrease/increase in the birth-rate, a decrease/increase in the death-rate and changes in immigration/emigration rates. For example an increase of one million in the size of the population because of an increase in the number of immigrant workers between the ages of 18 and 45 will have very different effects to a decrease in the death-rate resulting in one million more old-age pensioners.

Population measurement
The most important measures are
1 **Birth-rate** Measured as the number of live births per thousand of the population per year.
2 **Death-rate** Measured as the number of deaths per thousand of the population per year.
3 **Net migration** The difference between the totals of immigrants and emigrants, with '+' meaning a net increase in the population and '—' meaning a net decrease.
4 **Age distribution of the population** Highlights the changing proportions of young and old people.

Population problems
1 **Ageing population** the average age rises. This situation is caused by either (a) a decrease in the birth-rate, or (b) a decrease in the death-rate, or (c) a combination of both, or (d) a migration of young people. Britain's population has been ageing for many years.
2 **Declining population** the total size of the population falls. This situation is caused by either (a) the death-rate exceeding the birth-rate, or (b) emigration being greater than immigration. In the mid 1970s the decrease in the birth-rate in Britain pointed to a declining population to come by the end of the century, but in 1978 the birth-rate rose again.
3 **Increasing population** the total population increases because there is either (a) an increase in the birth-rate, or (b) a decrease in the death-rate, or (c) a combination of both, or (d) an increase in immigration. In modern times, this is usually associated with an ageing population.

The following is an example of the kind of examination question you you might see on this material.

1 Discuss the factors which determine the trend in the size of the United Kingdom population. (JMB)

The effects of an ageing population

1 As the population's average age increases, the proportion of old people increases. Fewer workers are supporting an increasing number of non-workers. The 'dependent' population increases. This will (a) increase the level of taxes needed to pay for pensions, health facilities etc., (b) reduce the national output, assuming the level of technology is unchanged.

2 The population will become less mobile (a) geographically – an older population is less likely to be willing to move around the country – and (b) occupationally – an older population is both less willing and less able to adopt new skills and trades.

3 There will be a shift in consumption patterns. Goods and services for young people, such as records and adventure holidays, will be in less demand, whereas goods and services for old people, such as medicines and chiropody, will be in greater demand. As a result, some industries will contract and others expand.

4 Labour will be in short supply and there may be tendencies towards (a) an increase in automation and mechanization, (b) an increase in real wages, and (c) a possible increase in the age of retirement.

5 Attitudes of businessmen and workers may be affected. Because older people are generally more conservative, there will be less new investment and risk taking. Thus, there will be fewer new products and less innovation. This could be the result of either a smaller market or a market with an increasing proportion of old people.

2 *Define (a) ageing population (b) optimum population.*
What are the economic consequences of an ageing population? (ox)

The effects of an increasing population

1 Increased population may lead to an increase in the size of the labour force. If the labour force becomes a higher percentage of the total population this may result in (a) increased national output, (b) reduced tax levels, because a smaller dependent population needs less expenditure per taxpayer on pensions and other services.

2 A reduction in the average age of the population will (a) increase labour mobility geographically and occupationally, (b) make less demands on some of the services of the welfare state, e.g. pensions and sick pay, (c) make greater demands on some of the services of the welfare state, e.g. maternity allowances and education, and (d) encourage innovation and enterprise because of natural youthful ambition.

3 If the increased population is a result of an increase in the birth-rate, there will be a shift in consumption patterns. Markets will be dominated by the needs and wants of young people, and industries will consequently be affected.

4 An increased market may encourage greater investment in the expectation of greater sales. If production does not keep pace with the growing market, inflation may occur as excess demand forces up prices.

5 If the rise in population happens when the country's resources are not fully exploited (under-population), a rise in the standard of living may result.

6 If the increase in population happens when the country's resources are being fully used (optimum population), production patterns will have to change to provide enough essential goods and services. Shortages in less essential things will result.

7 The effects of a population increase are not likely to be the same across the whole country: pollution, housing problems and traffic congestion will vary.

8 Increased population will not automatically lead to an increase in output. If the national output does not increase by the same percentage as the population increase, there will be a fall in the standard of living because more people will be sharing the national income cake. This may happen for a time if the increased population results from an increase in the birth-rate.

3 *What are the economic effects of changes in the distribution of population?* (WEL)

Examination preparation

Objective test study material

Prepare definitions for the following

Optimum population   Ageing population   Declining population
Under-population   Over-population   Birth-rate   Death-rate
Net migration   Dependent population   Working population

Factual information

You should be able to recognize figures which make sense for the following: Present UK population   Age distribution (broad categories)   Birth-rate   Death-rate

e.g. *Which is the best estimate of the population of the UK today?*

(a) 0.56 million
(b) 5.6 million
(c) 56 million
(d) 560 million

You should recognize that (c) is the correct answer.

Calculations From a table showing the age distribution of the population, calculate the size of the dependent population.

Diagrammatical material
Population data may be presented in various forms, e.g. statistical tables, pie charts, histograms. Usually two or more years are compared and what is required is to spot and sometimes explain significant changes.

Essay questions
Usually questions will centre on the effects of an increase or decrease in population. Perhaps the core of the question might be disguised – *what would be the social and economic effects of a rapid decline in population on the UK economy?* – but the basic information required by examiners will be the same. In all answers on this topic:
1 State that the effects will depend on the present size of the population in relation to the optimum population. This is not a fixed, absolute figure but depends on available factor resources and the level of technology.
2 State that the effects of population changes will depend on the reasons for change: increased birth-rate and decreased death-rate have differing effects, even though both may cause an increase in population.
3 Use these points selectively to answer the question. Few marks will be awarded for listing a whole series of effects of population growth/ decline unless the facts are marshalled in such a way as to answer the question directly.

The dependent population of Britain is increasing as a percentage of total population. What are the economic and social effects of this?

Para 1 Define dependent population, namely as that part of the population which is *not* part of the working population. The proportion can increase through
(a) increase in birth-rate
(b) raising of the school-leaving age, or increase in voluntary education beyond statutory leaving age
(c) decline in death-rate (important for Britain).

Para 2 Discuss the effects on public expenditure and revenue:
(a) proportionally fewer workers will be paying taxes; therefore there will be a need to increase levels of taxation.
(b) there will be an increase in public expenditure because of greater demands on the health service, pensions etc.

Paras 3–4 Discuss the effects on the working population.
(a) the proportion of the population working will be smaller at a given level of technology; output per head may fall
(b) there will be less occupational mobility – with its average age increased, the working population less able and less willing to learn new trades
(c) there will be less geographical mobility so the working population will be less able and less willing to move to other regions
(d) increase in real wages if demand for labour remains the same and supply falls – alternatively increased mechanization and automation.
(e) possibly increased retirement age (extend working life).

Paras 5–6 The effects on industrial activity should also be pointed out.
(a) shifts in consumption patterns will be reflected in decline of certain industries and expansion of others. Provide examples
(b) levels of investment may decline because of the consequent reduction in expected markets
(c) there will be less innovation and research and development.

Para 7 Social effects should also be raised in your answer.
(a) shifts in entertainment and holiday patterns will occur
(b) the crime rate may decline because of the different age structure
(c) there will be proportionally fewer marriages, therefore less demand for houses and schools.

Possible marking scheme
Para 1   3 marks for definition, 1 for comment.
Para 2   (a) 2 marks, (b) 2 marks.
Paras 3–4 (a) 2 marks, (b) 2 marks, (c) 2 marks, (d) 2 marks, (e) 1 mark.
Paras 5–6 (a) 2 marks, (b) 2 marks, (c) 1 mark.
Para 7   (a) 1 mark, (b) 1 mark, (c) 1 mark.
Note These marks total 25 but the maximum possible would be 20.
This answer makes reference to occupational and geographical mobility and to the working population. These topics will be discussed more fully in Chapter 7, 'Labour'.

What factors determine the efficiency of a country's labour force?

Note that this question is not concerned with the size of the workforce.

Any reference to the size of the workforce in your answer will earn no marks.

Section A Definition and measurement of labour efficiency
Para 1 Point out that efficiency is measured by productivity, output per man in a given time period. It is measured either by physical output, e.g. number of cars produced by each British Leyland worker/year, or by monetary value of each worker's output, the only method possible in service industries.

Section B Factors affecting efficiency of labour
Para 2 Discuss the role of capital stock, the type of equipment and degree of automation. You could illustrate this by an example. For instance, you could compare the productivity of Indian farming peasants with US farmers.
Para 3 Look at enterprise: how efficiently the workforce is organized, the role of management, the successful division of labour.
Para 4 What is the role of labour relations? Point out the importance of harmonious industrial relations, the effects of number of days lost through strikes and acceptance of new methods of production, especially labour-saving machinery.
Para 5 Discuss the effects of the age structure. A 'young' average age may go with readier acceptance of new techniques and technology, adaptability, energy, health, more incentives etc.
Para 6 Discuss the role of education. A better trained and educated workforce is more adaptable to change and new methods and therefore more efficient.
Para 7 Government policy will affect this through loans to firms, tax incentives to buy modern equipment, government research and development programmes, tax incentives to encourage greater production from workers etc.
Para 8 Here you may mention other factors such as working conditions affecting absenteeism or the health of the nation affecting efficiency.

Section C Importance of relationship between factors
Para 9 In your conclusion you should mention that output per person is dependent on a series of inter-related factors – for instance a massive capital expenditure on modern equipment will be no use unless the workforce is educated and trained to utilize the equipment and prepared to accept the changed conditions.

Possible marking scheme
The usual allocation of marks in a question of this nature is 1 mark for

mentioning a point. Then the additional mark or marks are given for a full explanation. A clear explanation is essential because examiners are given some freedom as to how many marks they award for expansion. It is for this reason that each point requires a separate paragraph.

Examination practice

4 *What would be the likely economic consequences of*
   (a) *a fall in birth-rate*
   (b) *increase in immigration*
   (c) *raising of the school-leaving age?*   (ox)
5 *What would be the economic effects of a fall in the birth-rate?*   (ox)

5 Location of industry

Synopsis The geographical distribution of industry in the UK is a significant factor affecting the overall level of economic activity. The reasons, often conflicting, which attract firms to certain regions must be studied. Regional imbalance is important and the reasons for it and possible measures to relieve it must be understood.

*

In the past the location of industry was often dictated by geographical factors which determined available power, source of raw materials and markets. Modern industry is to a large extent **footloose**. Because of changes in transport and communications and sources of power, there are often several alternative locations for factories which will give similar production costs.

In the eighteenth and nineteenth centuries various factors constrained businessmen in locating their factories. Thus, the early textile mills were situated in the Pennines for the water power located there; when steam power replaced water power, factories were set up near coalfields. It was a period when geographical factors (raw materials, power, climate, navigable estuaries) determined the location of industries. However, changes in transport and types of raw materials and new sources of power have given businessmen greater freedom in the siting of their factories. Industry today can often be located in many different areas without greatly increasing the costs of production. There are obvious exceptions: for example oil refining is best carried on near the coast where the material is imported or brought ashore. The cement industry is centred where supplies of chalk are readily available. A number of industries are **weight gaining** in that the weight and bulk of the finished product is greater than its raw materials - brewing and baking, for example – and it is economically sound for such industries to be situated near large markets.

Factors influencing location of factories (production units)

There are non-economic reasons for the location of industry; for instance a factory might be established because the owner lives in the area.
External economies are important in determining the location of industry: by setting up in a particular area, a firm is able to reduce its production costs. *Note* that the reduction in the costs of production is independent of the efficiency of the firm. It results simply because the firm is located in a particular area. These external economies may take several forms:

1 The existence of a skilled, trained labour force in the area. A pottery firm establishing itself in Stoke, or a cutlery firm in Sheffield, is able to take advantage of a pool of experienced labour without costs to itself.
2 The existence of a range of subsidiary industries in the area. In the Midlands many firms are to be found serving the car industries, e.g. Lucas. Technical colleges run courses particularly applicable to local industries and universities undertake research for particular industries.
3 The existence of specialist services serving an industry. These include accounting, marketing, advertising, warehousing, transporting, legal, banking. All will have developed expertise in the industry.
4 The area might be served by an efficient transport system. The South East, for example, is served by two major airports, is the focus of motorways and railways, has a modern port and easy access to the Channel ports. All of these obviously reduce the costs of transportation.
5 The area might contain a large market. There are obvious advantages for a firm processing food, for example, to be located in London, Birmingham or Manchester or any other conurbation.
6 Sometimes a firm will gain prestige (and therefore markets) by being located in a particular area, e.g. a firm making cutlery in Sheffield.
7 Land. Some industries need cheap land in large amounts.

These factors inter-relate and have a snowball effect. The more industry concentrates in an area, the more subsidiary firms, specialist services etc. develop, and this in turn attracts more firms in the industry to the area. The result is that certain area of UK have attracted 'footloose' industry and have experienced economic growth, whereas other areas have not only failed to attract new industries but have suffered from a decline of industries traditionally based in those areas, e.g. shipbuilding, textiles, iron and steel.

Here are two examples of examination questions on the determination of location of industry.

1 What factors affect
   (a) location of firms
   (b) concentration of industry? (LOND)
2 What external economies of scale attract firms to locate their businesses in certain areas? (JMB)

Regional problems

Since the 1920s Britain has suffered a regional imbalance. This has been caused by an uneven pattern of economic growth in different parts of the country. Some of the problems created include

1 High levels of unemployment in a number of regions, notably in the North East, the South West, parts of Wales, Clydeside and Northern Ireland. Associated with this unemployment are social problems such as poor housing conditions, lack of local amenities and a high crime rate.
2 A shift of population to areas of high employment. This also causes social problems, namely a shortage of housing, schools and health facilities.
3 When industry develops in particular areas labour can be in short supply. This results in
   (a) high minimum wages being offered to attract necessary labour: this increases production costs
   (b) **wage drift**, where the actual earnings greatly exceed minimum wage levels through bonus schemes, non-monetary benefits etc. This too increases the costs of production
4 When industry concentrates in limited areas **external diseconomies** may emerge, i.e. the costs of production increase for reasons totally independent of the efficiency of the firm. Thus, if land is in short supply, land prices increase and rates increase. Traffic congestion will

help to increase transport costs. If labour is in short supply labour costs will increase.

Government policy on location of industry

Since the 1930s governments have attempted to influence firms in deciding where to build new factories. Governments realize that firms usually favour locations where costs of production are at the lowest levels; that for a firm to build elsewhere increases its costs of production. But governments must consider the whole economy and seek to avoid the problems of imbalance stated above.

Compulsion or push measures
All major developments require an **Industrial Development Certificate** (IDC). If such a certificate is withheld, firms must then not expand *or* expand only in an area for which a certificate will be obtainable.

Persuasion or pull measures
Governments try to create 'artificial' external economies. Governments hope to offer inducements which will allow a firm to reduce its costs of production by building in a particular area. These inducements over the last decades have taken a variety of forms, both direct and indirect.

1 Regional employment premiums – the government pays a part of the workers' wages.
2 Training schemes in which workers are trained at the government's expense. This enables firms to acquire skilled labour without the expense of training.
3 The building of factories which are then sold or leased at most economical rates to firms.
4 Generous grants and tax allowances to firms in certain areas when they expand or purchase new equipment.
5 Development of an infrastructure such as a motorway programme which serves to encourage firms to establish in areas which were previously inaccessible.
6 Grants to local authorities. These enable local government to take steps to attract industry: for example, developing town centres, building industrial estates, embarking on a housing programme.
7 Conducting publicity campaigns to inform industry of the various attractions and economic advantages of regions outside the developing regions.

Implications of government intervention

1 If firms are persuaded to locate where costs are not at a minimum, then costs of production increase. This can make exports less competitive.
2 Social costs of industry may be reduced because there is less congestion, pollution, or the social services are not being over-stretched. On the other hand community services may be under-used: for example schools are often not fully utilized in declining regions.
3 Unemployment in regions causes a migration of the younger, more enterprising members of the community which results in further regional depression.
4 To achieve maximum economic growth all resources need to be fully utilized; this means all regions, not simply the South East and Midlands.
5 If regions continue to have high levels of unemployment, then the heavy government expenditure on welfare services will be a burden on the taxpayer.

Note There are strong political implications in regional policy reflected in the differences in attitudes of the major parties. Also the problem regions contain many of the marginal parliamentary seats. Consequently, the measures in force change frequently and students should try to keep up-to-date with current policies. You may well get a question on regional policy, for example:

3 *Outline the reasons for above average numbers of unemployed in certain regions of the UK. How have governments attempted to overcome this problem?* (WEL) (Amended)

Examination preparation

Objective test study material

Prepare definitions for the following
Footloose   External economies and diseconomies   Weight gaining and weight losing industries   Social costs   Wage drift   Pull and push measures

Factual information
You should be aware of which regions have high unemployment figures; and which regions are assisted by the government.

Diagrammatical material

You should be familiar with and able to interpret

(a) tables of regional unemployment levels
(b) tables showing employment opportunities
(c) tables showing levels of industrial activity in different regions.

Essay questions

Questions on location usually require

1 An ability to compare the term 'footloose' industry with the constraints on nineteenth-century industry.
2 Knowing that in the twentieth century concentration of industry in the Midlands and the South East has taken place.
3 Knowledge of the reasons for, and the effects of, this trend.
4 Knowledge of the reasons for, and the methods of, government intervention.

Why do governments seek to influence firms in locating their factories? What are the effects of this interference?

Note This question does not require a description of *how* a government tries to influence location. A detailed discussion along those lines will obtain no marks.

Para 1 Expand the theme that a majority of industry is 'footloose'. Also mention the exceptions.
Para 2 Discuss the major factor determining location, the external economies. Define and give examples of external economies.
Para 3 Discuss the consequences of external economies: concentration in the Midlands and the South East while other areas are declining in industrial importance. Mention the harmful social and economic effects of this trend.
Paras 4–7 In brief, separate paragraphs explain unemployment, social problems, inflationary effects and external diseconomies.
Para 8 To avoid these effects successive governments have sought to influence location. To evaluate this policy it is necessary to balance the possible increase in costs of production against the gains.
Paras 9–12 Explain in brief, separate paragraphs what is to be gained from regional policy: social costs, employment, economic growth and reduction in government expenditure.

Possible marking scheme
In an essay of this type where many points can be introduced, usually

1 mark is awarded for mentioning a valid point. Then 2 (sometimes 3) marks are awarded for expanding a point. Each of the paragraphs mentioned here could earn 2 marks.

Examination practice

4 *Explain the term 'localization of industry'. Why are some industries dispersed throughout the country while others are concentrated in one area?* (ox)

6 Production

Synopsis All economic activity results in the production of goods and services. Modern developed economies apply the principle of the **division of labour** to increase production. There are many ways of organizing production. An understanding of the ways in which the costs of production can be measured is important.

★

Production is the process by which commodities arrive at a final stage and are available to yield satisfaction to consumers. There is **direct production** in which consumers produce for their own needs, e.g. subsistence farming, and **indirect production** in which production is carried out by many workers and their output satisfies the needs of other consumers. This involves interdependence.

The chain of indirect production can be divided into

1 **Primary production** The **extraction** of basic or raw materials, e.g. fishing, mining, drilling for oil. About 3 per cent of the UK workforce is engaged in primary production. This percentage has declined in this century because of the exhaustion of supplies and cheaper sources abroad.

2 **Secondary production** The manufacture of **goods,** e.g. cars, clothes, tinned foods. About 42 per cent of the UK workforce is engaged in secondary production. This percentage has declined in recent years largely through the adoption of capital intensive methods of production.

3 **Tertiary production**
   (a) those services which help to bring the finished articles to the

consumer, e.g. transport, wholesaling, retailing, advertising, banking, insurance
(b) those services which help to increase the standard of living, e.g. hairdressing, entertainment, travel agents
(c) administration, e.g. civil service, police, armed forces.

Over 55 per cent of the UK workforce is engaged in the tertiary stage. This increase reflects a rise in the general standard of living, more leisure and increased state involvement in developing the welfare state.

Specialization and the division of labour

Production is characterized by specialization at all levels.

1 International Certain nations specialize in certain goods or services, e.g. oil producing countries, coffee producing countries, British insurance.
2 Regional Certain areas are noted for certain goods, e.g. Sheffield steel.
3 Industrial Companies may specialize in the production of certain goods. For instance, in the car industry various firms produce different components, e.g. Lucas.
4 Plant At this level the specialization in the productive process is known as the division of labour: each worker specializes in one particular task in the productive process, e.g. in the car industry. The division of labour is also found in services, e.g. law, teaching.

Advantages of the division of labour
1 Repetition of same task improves expertise.
2 Limited amount of training needed.
3 Specialist skills fully utilized, e.g. manual skills, numerate ability.
4 Less duplication of equipment, i.e. workers need a limited amount. of equipment.
5 Greater opportunities to use machinery.
The result is improved output and quality at lower costs.

Disadvantages of the division of labour
1 Repetition of same task results in boredom. This may lead to strikes.
2 Decline in skills and craftsmanship.
3 Interdependence of production can result in dislocations if one stage is held up.
4 Labour immobility, since workers are trained for only a limited range of jobs.

1 Describe the main advantages and disadvantages of specialization of labour. (JMB) (Amended)

Production takes place within the firm. In the firm the factors of production are combined, decisions on output levels etc. are made. There is an immense variety in the size of firms. Increasingly the economy is dominated by larger firms.

Reasons for the growth of firms
1 Larger units are often more efficient because of the economies to be derived from large-scale production.
2 Large firms may establish a dominant position (approaching monopoly) in the market.
3 Multi-product firms operating in many different markets reduce the risk of a fall in demand for one product, e.g. the tobacco companies.

Ways in which a firm may grow
1 Natural growth, i.e. internal expansion to increase production.
2 Merging or taking over. In this case two or more companies combine to form one larger company.
   (a) **vertical integration** one firm combines with another at a different stage of production. This may be either **backward** which is towards the supply of raw materials, ensuring a steady supply at a fixed quality and price, e.g. tyre firms buying a rubber plantation; or **forward** which is towards the consumer, ensuring selling outlets, after sales service etc., e.g. a car producer setting up dealerships.
   (b) **horizontal integration** one firm combines with another at the same stage of production, e.g. Peugeot/Renault. This may give economies of large-scale production or a greater dominance of the market.
   (c) **lateral integration** combining firms might have common sources of raw materials or market outlets but are not in direct competition, e.g. Schweppes and Cadbury's.

Here is an example of the type of essay question you may see on company mergers:

2 What are the main reasons for company mergers? (JMB)

Economies of scale

When production is organized on a large scale, the average cost of producing each unit of production is sometimes lower than when production is organized on a small scale. These economies, or savings in average cost, are of different kinds.

Technical or physical economies
1 Application of the division of labour increases output and decreases labour costs per unit.
2 Increases in volume of machinery and equipment requires a less than proportional increase in materials, e.g. steel required for a 500 gallon vat and for 1000 gallon vat.
3 Large throughput of production may justify using modern efficient machinery, which would not be fully used at lower levels of production.
4 Research and development departments can usually exist only in large organizations.
5 Where different stages of production have different optimum levels, matching is possible. For example a large farm may have four tractors, two ploughs and one combine harvester; a smaller one would have one of each but they would not all be fully utilized.

Marketing economies
1 Bulk buying often reduces unit cost and sometimes the bulk buyer can dictate standards of quality.
2 Selling costs, such as advertising and deliveries, have a lower average cost if spread over a large number of units.
3 Expert buyers and salesmen may be employed.

Financial economies
1 Large organizations may often borrow at lower interest rates than small firms.
2 Large firms have more sources of finances, including the Stock Exchange, available.

Risk-bearing economies
1 Demand in national or international markets is less likely to fluctuate than in small, local markets.
2 Large organizations may have the resources to withstand bad times caused by broken contracts, strikes, bad weather etc.
3 Insurance premiums do not rise in proportion to the sum insured.

Administrative economies
1 In manufacturing industry, as production increases, management and supervision do not have to increase at the same rate.

2 Large organizations which have many production plants or selling outlets may have one central administrative unit (head office).

3 Efficient, but expensive, systems, e.g. computers, microfilm, electronic data processing, may be used in large firms.

3 Describe clearly the internal economies of scale a firm may achieve.
(AEB) (Amended)

Diseconomies of scale

When production is organized on a large scale, areas exist where there are disadvantages in comparison with small-scale production. These may give higher average costs in some cases.

Organizational problems Too many layers of management may result in 'red-tape', slowing down the decision making process or failing to correct errors quickly.

Production problems Expensive machinery may be idle if sales orders do not match capacity. Waste of materials is likely without careful supervision.

Labour relations Industrial unrest, leading to strikes and other action, is more likely to occur in large organizations.

Customs relations Impersonal attitudes by employees may lose sales.

Costs

Costs of production may be examined in three ways.

Total costs are made up of **fixed costs,** i.e. those which do not alter as output changes, e.g. rent, rates, interest on loans etc. and **variable costs,** i.e. those which change as output changes, e.g. raw materials and labour.

Average costs (sometimes called **unit costs**) are calculated by dividing total costs at different output levels by the appropriate output. Because of the spreading of fixed costs over greater outputs, and also in cases where economies of scale exist, average costs often fall as output increases. If there are diseconomies of scale, average costs will increase after a certain output level. This diagrammatically gives a U-shaped average cost curve. The point of lowest average cost is called the **optimum** (most efficient) **output level.**

Marginal costs are the extra costs incurred or saved if output is increased or decreased by one unit. They are calculated by subtracting total costs at one output level from total costs at another level. Where there is a U-shaped average cost curve, the marginal cost curve is below the average cost curve when average cost is falling and above the average cost curve when average cost is rising. Marginal cost equals average cost at the optimum output level.

Cost information may be presented as either schedules, tables or curves.

Examination preparation

Objective test study material

Prepare definitions for the following
Primary production   Secondary production   Tertiary production
Division of labour   Diversification   Horizontal and vertical integration
Average cost   Marginal cost   Fixed and variable costs   Optimum level
Economies of scale   Diseconomies of scale

Diagrammatical material
You should be familiar with and able to interpret
(a) a table of production figures and work out the average cost or marginal cost and thus the optimum level of output (AC=MC)
(b) a table showing shifts of the working population between primary, secondary and tertiary sectors and be able to describe and explain the shifts.

To describe in words any such table usually obtains one-third to one-half of the total marks. All that is necessary is to express accurately in simple words the table *emphasizing the key words and figures*. For example, in discussing the *percentage* of working population engaged in tertiary sector, say it has increased by X per cent over the last ten years and *do not* give the *number* of workers engaged. Don't say there has been a drop of 1000 workers, when in fact the table is in thousands so what you should be writing is that there has been a drop of 1,000,000 workers. Put *all* the information down no matter how trivial and straightforward it might appear.

Describe the trend reflected in the following table. What reasons account for this trend?

Employment in manufacturing firms in the United Kingdom

	All firms (thousands)	Small firms (thousands)	Small firms as % of total
1948	6871	2538	37
1968	7870	2280	29

1 The description = 8 marks
   (a) the number employed in manufacturing industry increased from
       6,871,000 to 7,870,000   2 marks
   (b) the number employed in small firms decreased from 2,538,000
       to 2,280,000   2 marks
   (c) in 1948 37 per cent of workers in manufacturing industry worked
       for small firms. By 1968 this had fallen to 29 per cent   4 marks

Note Marks are easily obtained if care is taken. All detail must be
included.

2 Account for trend
   (a) increase in manufacturing production in the post-war period to
       meet increased consumer demand, at home and abroad   2 marks
   (b) mergers: horizontal, vertical, lateral   3 marks
       reasons for integration   (1 mark × 3 reasons)   3 marks
   (c) decline of small firm because of:
       bankruptcy in times of recession
       government policies – tax changes
       competition from larger firms
       increasing size of optimum firm   (1 mark × 4)   4 marks

Essay questions
The essays on these topics are usually straightforward, and though
occasionally disguised, simply require a descriptive approach.

*Although the advantages of the division of labour are economic the dis-
advantages are social. Discuss.*

This is a typical question. Basically the information required is a discussion of the advantages and disadvantages of the division of labour.

Para 1 Define division of labour and give an example. Say that this
results in increased production, an improved product and lower costs.
This is achieved by:
Para 2 Increased expertise. (Expand on this point.)
Para 3 Reduced training.
Para 4 Skills of workers being fully utilized.
Para 5 Increased automation.
2 marks × 3. One mark for reference. One mark for expansion.
Para 6 Refer to the many social disadvantages:
Boredom.
Less emphasis on training and education – labour immobility.
Unemployment and lay-offs affect living standards.

Paras 7–8 These disadvantages also have economic consequences:
Boredom results in strikes.
Economic dislocation.
Immobility of labour.

Possible marking scheme
You could gain 4 marks for the first paragraph, 2 marks for each of the two main points. Paras 2–5 are worth 2 marks each, one for reference and one for expansion, up to a total of 10 marks for this part of the question. The three points of advantages and disadvantages mentioned in paras 6–8 are worth 2 marks each up to a maximum of 10 marks.

Examination practice

4 Explain what is meant by economies of scale. Why might governments encourage the development of small firms? (LOND)

5 (a) With the use of examples, give a full explanation of each of the following terms:
(i) horizontal integration
(ii) vertical integration.
(b) Giving reasons explain whether the economy and the general public benefit from both types of integration. (RSA)

7 Labour

Synopsis The size and structure of the labour force is very important in determining the level of economic activity in an economy. There are many factors that affect the efficiency of the labour force. Changes in the patterns of employment, both nationally and regionally, and by industry, need to be examined.

*

To be able to produce goods and services, an economy must have certain resources which are sometimes called the **factors of production – labour, land, capital** and **enterprise.**

Labour and enterprise are the human resources. Originally, there seemed to be a clear distinction between manual workers, who contributed nothing but physical labour, and managers, who organized production and contributed only mental activity. Today, in many jobs this distinction is blurred. Another distinction is sometimes made between **employed** workers, which will include many managers, and **self-employed** workers, which will include many manual workers. It is more useful to think of the **labour force**, or **workforce**, as being the human resources available in an economy for economic activity.

The size of the labour force

The best definition of the UK's labour force is the total of those people over 16, possessing a National Insurance card, who are in employment or are seeking employment. Thus, the unemployed are part of the labour force. On this basis, the labour force of the UK is about twenty-five million, including ten million females.

Factors determining the size of the labour force
1 The total size of the population.
2 The minimum statutory school-leaving age.
3 The number of people in full-time education above the age of 16.
4 The age of retirement.
5 The number of people working beyond retirement age. This may be affected by the level of retirement pension available and by **earnings rules** for pensioners.
6 The number of housewives who are working. This is affected by changes in general attitudes to working wives and mothers and by attempts to gain higher standards of living.
7 The level of social security benefits available: certain earnings related benefits may deter people from working (see discussion on the **poverty trap** in Chapter 13).

Note   In addition to the size of the workforce, the number of hours worked and the number of holidays taken will be significant factors in determining the annual supply of labour in an economy. In recent years there have been important changes in these areas in the UK.

The efficiency of the labour force

The size of the labour force is not as economically important as its efficiency. The emphasis today is on labour **productivity**, i.e. how much each worker can produce.

Factors determining the efficiency of the labour force
1 The equipment (**capital**) used by the labour force.
2 The level of education of the workforce. (As technology becomes more complex, workers must have a high level training to maximize efficiency.)
3 The efficiency of organization, i.e. is management making the best use of human resources?
4 Industrial relations, management attitudes. Good relations reduce strikes and allow technological change to take place.
5 Industrial relations, trade union attitudes – whether to accept redundancies through adoption of modern technology or to resist change; the extent to which demarcation is enforced.
6 The health of the labour force.
7 The age pattern of the labour force.
8 Working conditions. Efficient lighting, heating and other environmental factors can in certain circumstances increase production levels.

Labour mobility

Occupational mobility

The ability of workers to move from one occupation to another. This mobility is becoming increasingly important as the speed of technological change quickens and some industries need to expand and others to decline.

Obstacles to occupational mobility

1 Natural abilities, e.g. the intelligence required to become a doctor or the physical strength and stamina required to become a miner.
2 Long periods of training. Men and women aged over 30 will find it very difficult to undertake a course of training without substantial financial assistance.
3 Lack of financial inducement. In some occupations, new entrants, regardless of age, start on a low wage or salary and it takes several years for them to reach a worthwhile figure.
4 Age. Possible employers will not train workers if their remaining working life is short.
5 Trade unions. In many trades where a **closed shop** operates, a worker cannot be employed without a union card which is not readily given.
6 Personal reasons:
   (a) some workers prefer to remain unemployed and wait for an opening in their last occupation, rather than change jobs.
   (b) alternative occupations might be considered undesirable, e.g. vacancies may exist in the armed forces, the Post Office and London Transport even though there are one and a half million unemployed.
   (c) ignorance – people may be unaware of vacancies in other industries or of the qualifications needed or training available.

Ways of increasing occupational mobility

1 Retraining programmes organized by the government with assistance to workers undertaking them.
2 Increased information – perhaps through local jobcentres or government advertising.

Here is an example of the type of essay question you may see on occupational mobility:

1 What is meant by occupational immobility of labour? How can the government increase the occupational mobility of labour? (ox) (Amended)

Geographical mobility

Geographical mobility is the ability or willingness of workers to move about the country in search of employment. This is important because different regions in the UK vary in job opportunities.

Obstacles to geographical mobility

1 Family reasons. These could include the loss of friends, the existence of dependent relatives, problems associated with changing schools or the jobs of the other working members of the family.
2 Expenses. This involves the costs of buying and selling a house and removal expenses.
3 Accommodation. For those who do not own their own house rented accommodation is scarce; local authorities normally allocate council houses to those who have been on the waiting list the longest.
4 Prejudice. Many industrialized areas are considered undesirable to live in, because of congestion and pollution, even though employment opportunities exist there.
5 Ignorance. Sometimes there is just simply a lack of knowledge of employment opportunities in other parts of the country.
6 Lack of financial inducement. Sometimes there is no incentive to search for work in other parts of the country because of the levels of unemployment and social security benefits and tax rates on wages.

Ways of increasing geographical mobility

1 Grants from local or central government to assist in removal expenses.
2 Provision of hostel and other accommodation.
3 Provision of travel warrants for workers separated from their families.
4 Spreading of information about job opportunities.

Note It must be said that none of these measures has been very successful. Here is a more general question about the mobility of labour.

2 What is meant by immobility of labour? What are the main reasons for the immobility of labour? How, if at all, can they be overcome? (OX)

Occupational distribution of the labour force

1 Primary sector (first stage or extractive industries): this includes mining, quarrying, drilling, farming, forestry and fishing.
2 Secondary sector (manufacturing and construction): this involves transforming raw materials into products.
3 Tertiary sector (services): this includes all commercial occupations,

banking, insurance, transport, retailing etc. and all direct services, hairdressing, undertaking, teaching etc.

Changes in occupational distribution

	1911 (%)	1978 (%)
Primary	14	3
Secondary	38	38
Tertiary	47	53
Armed Forces ⎫ Unemployed ⎭ 1		6

Comment

1 Primary sector. There has been a marked decline because of an increasing switch to mechanization, in other words capital being substituted for labour, e.g. combine harvester; the exhaustion of natural resources, e.g. tin and copper mining, fishing in some areas; and labour attracted away from the primary sector into secondary and tertiary sectors.

2 Secondary sector. Within this sector there are constant shifts as some industries expand and others decline. In the recent past, the percentage engaged in this sector has been much higher; there is now a decrease, which will probably continue, because of a switch to more capital intensive productive methods.

3 Tertiary sector. The increase here reflects an improved general standard of living, e.g. more leisure activities; development of the welfare state, e.g. social workers; increasing complexity in modern industry, e.g. more accountants, lawyers, and all the other types of consultant needed.

3 (a) *Describe the changes in the occupational distribution of population in the UK since 1960.*

(b) *What changes in the distribution can be expected over the next twenty years, and why?* (LOND)

Examination preparation

Objective test study material

Prepare definitions for the following

Labour intensive   Productivity   Occupational mobility   Geographical

mobility   Primary industries   Secondary industries   Tertiary industries

Factual information
You should have an idea of the broad figures involved: percentages of
working population in each sector; size of labour force; number of
females in labour force etc.

Diagrammatical material
Statistical tables and pie charts or histograms may be used to present
some basic data. Usually two or more years, or regions, are compared
and recognition and interpretation of important differences are required.

Essay questions
Essay questions relating to this part of the syllabus usually ask for factual
information about changes in the size and composition of the labour
force, and examiners expect you to be able to give reasons for the changes
and the economic effects of them.

*Why is occupational mobility of labour considered so important? What
problems face workers wishing to change their occupations half way through
their careers?*

Para 1 You should point out that the economy is always changing its
pattern of economic activity and the two important consequences of this
for labour – namely some industries are declining in importance, e.g.
ship-building, while other industries are expanding, e.g. North Sea oil
– and technological changes result in more mechanization/automation –
capital replacing labour causes redundancies.

Para 2 Continue by saying that the result of these developments is unemployment in some industries and employment opportunities in others.
If workers could transfer easily then there would be no major economic
problem, but there are many obstacles to workers changing jobs. (*Note*
This question refers to occupational, *not* geographical, mobility. While it
might be mentioned as a factor preventing a worker changing his job, if it
means moving to another area, *no* marks will be given for a digression on
geographical mobility.)

Paras 3–8 Each of these paragraphs should be devoted to a discussion
of the limitations to occupational mobility and examples given. The
following barriers should be mentioned: training (problems for workers
and employers), starting salary, age problems, attitudes of trades unions
and personal reasons for unwillingness to change jobs.

Para 9 Refer to government attempts to increase occupational mobility and comment on their effectiveness.

Possible marking scheme
Paras 1–2 are worth 3 marks each. Paras 3–8 are worth 1 mark each for naming a problem and up to a further 2 marks may be gained for explaining why it is a problem and giving an appropriate example. Para 9 should be worth 2 marks.

Note The maximum marks awarded will be 20, even though more marks are apparently available. The second part of the question carries more marks than the first, but development of points in the second part should bring out the importance of occupational mobility.

8 Unemployment

Synopsis Unemployment is a waste of human resources in an economy. It is necessary to define unemployment, to be able to recognize different types of unemployment and to examine the possible policies available to governments in dealing with the problem. It is also important to understand the consequences which may follow attempts to cure unemployment.

*

When the number of workers out of work exceeds the number of vacancies a situation of **unemployment** is said to occur. The number of registered unemployed is announced regularly each month. This figure is not completely accurate but it does give a broad indication of the number out of work and actively seeking a job. The figure is inaccurate for a number of reasons:

1 A number of adults are seeking work but do not register, e.g. housewives.
2 School-leavers remain at school becuase no jobs are available.
3 A number of adults register but are not really seeking employment, e.g. the work-shy and those retired early by their firms with little time before they reach pensionable age.
4 A number, albeit small, are in work but registered as unemployed.

The government has accepted responsibility for the maintenance of high employment levels. Some level of unemployment is accepted as inevitable because of the pattern of economic activity:

1 **Seasonal unemployment,** e.g. hotel trade.
2 Workers in the process of changing jobs, **transitional unemployment. (Frictional unemployment.)**
3 **Residual unemployment,** workers unfit for various reasons to take on the responsibility of a full-time job.

Having accepted responsibility for maintaining high employment levels, governments intervene in the economy to achieve this goal. The policies the government adopts will depend on the type of unemployment.

Structural unemployment

A shift in demand patterns or an increase in foreign competition can cause the rapid decline of an industry, e.g. textiles (foreign competition); shipbuilding (foreign competition and decline in demand); iron and steel (foreign competition and exhaustion of supplies). *Often* these industries have been concentrated in particular areas. The unemployment thus caused is **regional unemployment**. Structural and regional unemployment are therefore regarded as synonymous although this is not necessarily the case.

The problem has been compounded by the fact that the newer industries have not naturally established themselves in these areas but have concentrated elsewhere. This problem has been discussed in Chapter 5, but the policies of governments can be restated briefly.

The object is to attract industry to areas of high unemployment. This can be achieved by:

1 'Pull' factors – grants, loans, factories built, allowances, motorway network, Regional Employment Premiums etc.
2 'Push' factors – Industrial Development Certificates.
3 The 'spread' of government offices – Cardiff, Bootle, Newcastle.
4 Attractions offered by local authorities.
5 Obtaining grants from the European Economic Community.
6 Reducing import levels of particular goods, e.g. textile quotas.

Technological unemployment

Technological unemployment is a situation where workers become unemployed because of mechanization. Industries become more **capital intensive**, less **labour intensive**. Thus, as containerization was adopted by the ports, dockers became redundant; as automatic telephone exchanges were introduced, operators became redundant. These **redundancies** are inevitable as modern techniques are adopted by industry. Although often resisted by trade unions in an attempt to safeguard jobs, this only slows up the process and does not stop it.

To reduce the effects of this type of unemployment governments have

1 Established re-training centres and introduced a variety of grants to workers prepared to learn new trades.
2 Established jobcentres to enable workers to find new positions.
3 Assisted workers to move to areas where job opportunities exist.

General or cyclical unemployment

A situation where workers in a wide variety of trades and industries become unemployed throughout the country. This unemployment is caused by a fall in **aggregate demand**; that is, less is demanded both of capital goods and consumer goods and services. As less is demanded, less is produced, fewer workers are required, and workers become unemployed.

To reduce the level of unemployment the government must seek to increase demand for both consumer and capital goods.

Measures to increase demand for consumer goods

If people have more money to spend it is likely that they will show a greater demand for consumer goods. The government can give people more money by increasing the amount of its transfer payments – e.g. family allowances and old age pensions – or by reducing the levels of personal taxation. It has been found that if lower income groups are given an increase in real income, then a high percentage of the money will be spent on consumer goods and services. The government can also increase demand by increasing the availability of, and reducing the cost of, loans and overdrafts and making it easier to buy on credit.

Measures to increase demand for capital goods

Increased public expenditure Government spending on roads, houses etc. immediately results in more workers employed. It has a snowball effect in that incomes earned will be spent on consumer goods, thus generating more employment.

Encouraging firms to invest This can be done by reducing levels of corporation tax, giving tax concessions against investment and stimulating consumer expenditure. There are two major problems which arise from stimulating aggregate demand in this way: demand pull inflation (see Chapter 12 on 'Inflation') and a balance of payments deficit which comes about because the increased total demand will include increased demand for imported goods – consumer goods, raw materials etc.; inflationary effects will adversely affect export prices; and in a buoyant home market producers tend to ignore the export market.

Thus governments must strike a balance between stimulating the economy to create job opportunities and controlling possible inflation and a balance of payments deficit.

The following questions are typical of the essay questions set on this part of the syllabus:

1 (a) *What is unemployment?*
  (b) *What suggestions have been made regarding its causes?* (LOND)
2 *Explain the following types of unemployment:*
  (a) *seasonal*
  (b) *structural*
  (c) *frictional.* (WEL)
3 *Distinguish between*
  (a) *structural unemployment*
  (b) *cyclical unemployment. What measures can the government take to combat a recession in the economy?* (AEB)

Examination preparation

Objective test study material
Prepare definitions for the following
Unemployment   Seasonal unemployment   Structural unemployment
Technological unemployment   Cyclical unemployment   Residual
unemployment   Capital intensive   Labour intensive   Redundancy
Aggregate demand

Diagrammatical material
You should be able to deal with a question involving tables showing levels of employment in different industries or regions at different times and requiring explanation of causes.

Essay questions
The essay questions in this area are usually descriptive in nature and simply call for an understanding of the major causes of unemployment and possible policies to cure the problem of inflation. An awareness of the difficulties and problems involved, plus the limitations of government policies, will usually gain extra marks.

What policies have successive governments adopted to reduce the general level of unemployment?

This type of question reflects the fact that it is impossible to write at length on all the policies adopted by governments to reduce unemployment. The question refers specifically to general unemployment; thus no marks will be given for material which refers exclusively to seasonal, structural and technological unemployment. Occasionally a question might refer to all types of unemployment: this is perhaps a poor question but obviously must be answered by referring to all the different methods adopted by governments. Naturally only a superficial treatment will be required. This is the sort of organization you might aim for.

Para 1 Provide a definition of general unemployment. Explain its cause and refer to aggregate demand in doing so.

Para 2 Explain why the aim of government policies is to stimulate aggregate demand.

Para 3 Explain how to increase demand for consumer goods by increasing real incomes.

Para 4 Describe how consumer goods sales may be increased by increasing the availability of credit. Policies to do this include reducing interest rates and easing credit restrictions.

Para 5 Expand fully on the arguments about increasing public expenditure as a means of combating unemployment.

Para 6 Talk about the need for and means of encouragement of private investment, e.g. taxes, stimulating the market.

Para 7 Do point out that some unemployment cannot be successfully eradicated; at least 2 per cent is residual and transitional. There is a constant situation of certain industries declining. Moreover, a policy of increasing aggregate demand cannot be pursued in an unrestrained fashion because this will result in problems of inflation and balance of payments deficit.

Possible marking scheme
This type of question is extremely broad. It is, therefore, difficult to suggest a marking scheme. Perhaps the best guide is to state that probably up to 4 marks will be given for each major policy discussed. In addition marks will be awarded for definition and pointing out the need for restraints on policies.

Examination practice

4 *Describe the economic policies with which the government attempts to control unemployment in the UK.* (JMB)

5 (a) *Explain the causes of the following types of unemployment:*
    (i) *cyclical or mass unemployment*
    (ii) *frictional unemployment*
    (iii) *structural unemployment.*
  (b) *Suggest possible remedies for each of the above types of unemployment.* (RSA)

9 Wages and trade unions

Synopsis Economic theory suggests a pattern of wages that would emerge in a free market economy. The pattern in the real world, however, differs from the theoretical one; it is important to understand why this is so and to assess the importance of trade unions in affecting wage levels, and to know about the wider activities of trade unions.

*

In a planned economy the level of wages paid to industrial workers is determined by the state. In a free enterprise economy the market forces of supply and demand for labour will determine the wage (price) level for labour, as it does for all other goods.

Wages

In Britain wages are determined partly by supply and demand, that is market forces, and partly by the policy of the government and attitudes of trade unions.

Factors governing supply of labour for a particular occupation

1 The size of the labour force. This is affected by births and deaths, by immigration and emigration and by legislation determining the school-leaving and retirement ages.
2 The degree of natural skill and ability required. For example, brain surgeons who require a combination of intellectual ability and manual dexterity will always be in short supply, but the skills required by a shop assistant are minimal so therefore there is a ready supply.
3 The length of training required. For example, if there is a massive increase in the demand for solicitors the supply will not be increased for five or six years because that is the period of training required

for the job. The same principle applies to pilots, doctors, etc.
4 The attractiveness of the job. Some 'glamour' jobs such as airline pilots and professional footballers have a very high potential supply; others such as miners and refuse collectors have a low potential supply. This attractiveness is affected by hours worked, conditions of work, fringe benefits, status etc.

Factors governing the demand for labour in a particular occupation

1 Labour is a **derived demand**, therefore changes in the demand for a product caused by changes in fashions or a successful advertising campaign will affect the demand for labour to produce that product.
2 In a free enterprise economy, firms employ labour so that they may produce goods and services and sell them for a profit. Therefore labour will be employed up to the point where the value of the last man's output equals his cost to the firm (wages). This is known as the **marginal productivity theory** of wages.
3 The possibility of replacing labour with capital. If machines can do the work of men, then there comes a point when increases in wages make labour more expensive than machinery and the demand for labour will fall.
4 Certain industries are labour-intensive, that is, by their very nature, a high proportion of costs are labour costs simply because machines are unable to replace labour – e.g. teaching, hotels, hospitals, postal services. The demand for labour in money terms, i.e. wages offered, will be less than if labour forms a very small proportion of total costs, e.g. North Sea oil drillers.

This theoretical approach can sometimes explain the effects of wage levels on the demand for, or supply of, labour in particular occupations, e.g. pay increases affecting recruitment to the police or armed services and high wages in the car and dock industries encouraging the move towards automation. But this approach cannot explain the full pattern of wages in the UK today.

Two major influences distort the theoretical market model.

Trade unions

Trade unions affect the supply of labour either by obtaining and enforcing a **closed shop** policy, by which all employees doing certain jobs must be members of a particular trade union, or by having a sufficiently high proportion of union members in a workforce, so that by acting together they can exercise power in negotiations with employers.

Effects of trade unions on supply of labour

1 Sustaining an increase, or preventing a decrease, in the number of jobs for union members by insisting on agreed manning levels
2 Improving the bargaining position of workers in wage negotiations by industrial action or the threat of it. The tools of industrial action include:
   (a) **strikes** – total withdrawal of labour for a period
   (b) measures to reduce productivity – **overtime ban, go-slow, working-to-rule**, withdrawal of 'goodwill' etc.

As a result of trade union pressure, wages in some industries are higher than free market forces would indicate.

The policy of government

Since the early 1960s governments have increasingly attempted to influence the level of wage increases. Incomes policies in various forms (see Chapter 12) and strong persuasive methods have been used. These have been, in the main, applied to all industries and to all workers, completely ignoring the varying conditions of demand and supply of labour in particular industries.

Factors determining wage levels in UK today

1 Proportion of labour cost to total costs. Where labour costs are relatively low employers will often 'give in' to wage demands to avoid lost production.
2 Elasticity of demand for product. Wage demands will be more readily granted if increased costs can be passed on in higher prices without a significant fall in demand.
3 Profit record of industries. Industries making high profits are likely to be pressured to give wage increases.
4 Essential nature of industry. In industries crucial to the economy, e.g. coal, gas and electricity, industrial action can influence public opinion to push employers to grant wage demands.
5 Strength of trade unions. Well organized unions with many members in the workforce can push for high pay awards.
6 Social justice. Public opinion may urge government action to increase certain wages, e.g. nurses.
7 Differentials. This is the difference between the wages of one group of workers and another, usually those in the same industry falling into the broad groups of skilled, semi-skilled and unskilled. Demands for increases for one group are based on what has happened to another group, regardless of economic circumstances, e.g. a

10 per cent increase for skilled workers because of increased productivity may lead to a demand for 10 per cent for unskilled workers although there has been no parallel increase in productivity. Here are two questions typical of what you may see on wages on the essay paper:

1 Why do wage rates differ in different occupations? (ox)
2 Account for the fact that doctors earn more than bus conductors. (jmb)

The following terms used in discussing wages are ones with which you should be familiar.

Real wages and money (nominal) wages As the name suggests, money wage is simply the wage expressed in terms of amounts of money. Thus a worker on £50 might receive a 5 per cent increase i.e. £2.50 in his money wages, making his new money wage £52.50. Real wage is the amount of goods and services that can be purchased with the money wages. In our example, if prices had increased by 10 per cent, then the worker on £50 a week would need £55 to be able to buy the same amount of goods and services as before. If his increase is only 5 per cent (£2.50), his real wage will have fallen.

Economic rent This is income received over and above that which is necessary to keep a factor of production (usually labour) in its present use. It is payment for special talents or abilities which are in short supply relative to the demand for them. For example, a footballer receiving £500 per week might be prepared to play for £100 per week – below that figure he would take another job instead of playing football. The difference between what he gets and the least he would be prepared to accept (£400) is called economic rent. The remainder (£100) is called **transfer earnings.**

Wage drift The majority of workers have an **agreed minimum wage.** However, their gross pay or earnings can be considerably higher than the agreed minimum because of bonus schemes, commission, meal allowances etc. The difference between the gross earnings and wage rate is known as wage drift. This is found particularly in areas where there is a shortage of skilled labour.

Piece rate and time rate Time rate is a system of payment by which workers receive an agreed sum for every hour worked, e.g. a worker on £1.50 per hour for a forty-hour week will receive £60 (gross). Different rates may be agreed for overtime, shift work or other special circumstances. Piece rate relates payment to output or productivity, e.g. a worker paid 60p per finished garment will receive £60 if 100 garments are finished.

Advantages of piece rate

1 It acts as an incentive to greater effort and rewards efficiency.
2 It means that workers do not need to be strictly supervised because it is in their own interests to work to the maximum output.
3 Costs of production can easily be calculated because labour costs per article are known.
4 In many occupations boredom is a major factor. Payment by piece rate is a recompense in that high output results in high rewards.

Problems of applying piece rate

1 In some industries production needs to vary with demand, therefore maximum output is not always required.
2 Some jobs do not have a measurable output per worker.
3 Disputes arise about how much should be paid per article produced.
4 Quality deteriorates because speed becomes the workers' criterion and so a system of quality control is needed.
5 Industrial unrest occurs if there are any delays in the process of production.
6 Workers demand expensive machinery which is not always carefully maintained.

If these problems exist then there is a case for some form of time rate, but if time rate is used, then the benefits of piece rate cannot be obtained. Here is an example of the sort of question you may be set on this part of the syllabus:

3 What are the relative merits and demerits of time rate and piece rate as methods of wage payments? (JMB)

Gross wages and net wages Gross wages are the amount earned by a worker before stoppages such as income tax and national insurance contributions. Net wages are the amount earned after these stoppages – also called take-home pay.

Trade unions

Trade unions are not only concerned with wages. They also improve and maintain conditions of work; safeguard jobs against redundancies; provide social benefits to members (such as death grants); represent workers on bodies such as administrative tribunals and wage councils; and influence social and economic policies of government, either as separate unions or through the TUC.

Types of unions

1 **Craft unions** Often long established with membership restricted to skilled workers. The existence of craft unions makes wage bargaining for an entire industry difficult. In addition having different unions representing workers in the same industry creates demarcation disputes.

2 **Industrial unions** Membership is open to all workers in one industry, skilled and unskilled, e.g. National Union of Mineworkers.

3 **General union** Membership includes workers in different trades and industries, skilled and unskilled. Because they are usually large and cover such a wide range of interests, they are difficult to organize, e.g. Transport and General Workers' Union.

4 **White collar unions** Membership is restricted to non-manual workers, e.g. bank clerks, civil servants and teachers.
This type of union reflects the success of other unions and the pressures of inflation, e.g. Association of Scientific, Technical and Managerial Staff.

Union organization

Most trade unions have very similar organizations.

1 Plant and factory level. Union activity here is organized by an unpaid **shop steward** who negotiates at factory level with management.

2 Local units – **branch level.** Members from firms elect regional and national delegates who represent them in dealing with local issues.

3 **Union conferences** elect national executive and determine national policy.

4 **National Executive,** often dominated by the **General Secretary,** interpret union policy throughout the year.

Union weapons

Official strike This is a strike called by the union executive.

Unofficial strike is one called at factory level usually by the shop steward(s) without executive approval.

Work-to-rule This involves a ban on overtime, and employees work in accordance with strict procedures.

Closed shop Only union members are allowed to work in the firm involved.

Picketing This is a measure where some workers try to persuade other workers not to enter a firm to work during a strike period.

Here is an example of the sort of question set on this part of the syllabus:

4 Describe the main functions of trade unions. Give two recent examples
of union activity which have affected the economic life of the United
Kingdom? (WEL)

Employers' federations/associations

These are organizations representing the major firms in an industry. Their main function is to represent the employers' side in collective bargaining with unions to determine a basic national wage rate. Employers' Federations provide a range of services including giving advice on modern developments in industry and on problems of redundancy and taking part in negotiations with government and other bodies.

Examination preparation

Objective test study material

Prepare definitions for the following

Piece rate   Time rate   Money wages   Real wages   Economic rent
Wage drift   Gross wages   Net wages

Diagrammatical material

You should be familiar with and able to interpret tables showing changing patterns of differentials.

Essay questions

What factors determine the success of a trade union when pressing for a
substantial wage increase?

Para 1 In your introductory paragraph you should make the point that theoretically wage levels are determined by the supply and demand for labour. Give an example to show that to a certain extent this is still true; for instance, the limited availability of doctors and the constant demand will always ensure a reasonably high wage for doctors. But, conversely, trade unions can in certain circumstances achieve a higher award for their members than market forces merit.

Para 2 Point out that when the industry is a 'key' industry, e.g. one such as electricity or road transport, the community is immediately affected, whereas if social workers or probation officers were to take strike action, most people wouldn't notice.

Para 3 Explain that when a firm is making high profits, wage increases can obviously be paid out. However, this may well only be applicable to some firms within an industry, e.g. Ford workers could expect higher wage awards than their fellow workers at British Leyland.

Para 4 Describe the situation if there is an inelastic demand for the product or service. Thus, no matter how much essential services and products increased in price, demand would hardly fall: workers are therefore more able to press for higher wages.

Para 5 Also describe the case for popular support for workers in an industry. For example, miners, nurses etc. usually have the people's support when putting in claims for wage increases.

Para 6 If there is a closed shop, 100 per cent union support, or if workers are concentrated in factories (unlike farm labourers who are not in close physical proximity) then the success of industrial action – strikes etc. – will be more likely.

Para 7 Point out that in the case of capital intensive industries, when a firm is likely to sustain heavy losses when only a small percentage of its total cost is at stake, then wage demands are more likely to be successful.

Para 8 Discuss what happens if there is no government interference. Point out that in recent years governments have tried to keep wage awards down – through pay freezes, wage guidelines, etc. – both by statutory means and by broad advice backed up by the threat of withholding government contracts if the suggested limits were exceeded.

Possible marking scheme
For this question the introductory paragraph would be worth 2 marks while each subsequent paragraph would be worth a maximum of 3 marks – 1 mark for making the point and 2 points for expanding it.

Examination practice

5 *What is meant by real wages? Explain with suitable illustrations the main factors affecting the power of unions in pressing for wage increases.* (AEB)

10 Demand, supply and price

Synopsis An understanding of the working of market forces – supply and demand – is basic to any study of economics. Supply and demand must first be studied in a theoretical, 'unreal' situation, and once understood these principles can be applied to 'real world' situations to help understand the theory of price determination.

*

Demand

Demand is the term used to describe the quantity of a good or service which buyers are prepared to buy at a given price. For demand to exist, the good or service must have **utility** for the buyer, the buyer must have the means (money) to meet the price, and the buyer must be prepared to use his means to obtain the good or service.
Note Demand does not mean that all would-be buyers are necessarily able to get the quantity they would like, e.g. Cup Final tickets.
Demand schedule This is a table showing how much demand there is for a good or service at different price levels.
Demand curve This is a graphical representation of a demand schedule, where price is plotted on the vertical axis and quantity demanded is plotted on the horizontal axis.

All demand schedules and curves assume:
1 That the income of the potential buyers remains the same
2 That the prices of other goods, which have any close connection with the good concerned, remain the same

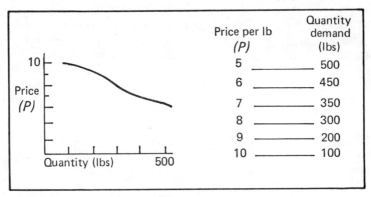

Price per lb (P)	Quantity demand (lbs)
5	500
6	450
7	350
8	300
9	200
10	100

3 That the tastes of the buyers and the fashionability of the good remain the same

4 That the size of the market, i.e. the number of potential buyers, remains the same.

In other words, a demand schedule or curve shows how demand would react to a change in *price* only; all other possible variables affecting the buying situation are assumed to be unchanged.

'Normal' demand Most commodities follow the general rule that if price goes up, less will be demanded and if price goes down, more will be demanded. This is what is known as normal demand. This is shown on a demand curve by a curve sloping downward from left to right.

Exceptional demand The demand for some commodities decreases when prices fall. These are known as **inferior goods**: they are bought only because buyers cannot afford better alternatives, e.g. bus travel. In other cases demand may rise when price goes up because buyers expect further price rises, e.g. shares.

Extension of demand This refers to an increase in quantity demanded resulting from a change in price. This is shown as a movement *along* the existing demand curve.

Contraction of demand This refers to a decrease in the quantity demanded resulting from a change in price. This is also shown as a movement *along* the existing demand curve.

Shift in demand If any of the basic assumptions on which the demand schedule/curve rests are altered, then a *new curve* is drawn, e.g. if the income of potential buyers increases, they may be prepared to buy more at all price levels.

Elasticity of demand

Elasticity of demand is a measure of the extent to which the quantity demanded varies when one of the factors affecting demand varies.

Price elasticity of demand Measures the extent to which demand for a commodity varies when price varies. It is calculated by the formula:

$$\frac{\% \text{ change in quantity}}{\% \text{ change in price}}$$

Income elasticity of demand Measures the extent to which demand for a commodity varies when income of potential buyers varies. It is measured by the formula:

$$\frac{\% \text{ change in quantity demanded}}{\% \text{ change in income}}$$

Cross elasticity of demand Measures the extent to which demand for one particular commodity varies when the price of another commodity varies. It is measured by the formula:

$$\frac{\% \text{ change in quantity of commodity } X}{\% \text{ change in price of commodity } Y}$$

All measurement of elasticity gives a figure ranging from 0 to infinity. A measurement of 0 means that there is no response in the quantity demanded to any change in the other variable being measured. A measurement of infinity means that the smallest possible change in the variable being measured results in an infinitely large change in the demand for the commodity. If the measurement gives a figure of less than one, demand is said to be **inelastic.** If the figure given is more than one, demand is said to be **elastic.** If the figure is exactly one, then demand is said to have **unitary elasticity**, i.e. a change in the variable affecting demand will bring about an exactly proportional change in demand: for example a 5 per cent change in income for would-be buyers of sweets may result in a 5 per cent change in the demand for sweets.

Factors determining price elasticity of demand

Note In studying economics at 0 level, the emphasis is on price elasticity rather than any of the other forms.

1 The proportion of income spent on the commodity. For instance a 20 per cent increase in the price of matches will have less effect

on demand than a 20 per cent increase in the price of coffee.

2 The extent to which the commodity is regarded as essential. Compare the effects of a 20 per cent increase in electricity prices with a 20 per cent increase in the price of brown boots.

3 The availability of substitutes or acceptable alternatives for the commodity. Where there is a very close substitute, as with different brands of tea, the demand for any one brand will be very elastic.

4 The durability of the commodity. If replacement purchases can be postponed by making do with goods purchased in the past, e.g. second-hand cars or new clothes, then demand will be elastic in comparison with the demand for purchases which cannot be postponed, e.g. school textbooks.

Other aspects of demand

Complementary demand Sometimes the demand for one commodity necessarily affects the demand for another commodity, e.g. tennis rackets and tennis balls; this is also sometimes called **joint demand**.

Competitive demand Where commodities are close substitutes for one another a change in the demand for one will affect the other in the opposite way, e.g. an increase in the demand for 'pop' cassettes may result in a decrease in the demand for 'pop' records.

Composite demand   Sometimes a commodity may have several different uses and therefore there will be several markets making up total demand, e.g. steel.

Derived demand In many cases, especially with commodities which are raw materials, the demand for the commodity depends on the demand for the final product, e.g. bauxite and aluminium.

Supply

Supply is the term used to describe the quantity of a good or service which sellers are prepared to sell at a given price. When discussing supply, the time factor is very important.

Market supply means that supply cannot be increased at all, e.g. apples on a street trader's barrow. **Short-term supply** allows the possibility of an increase in supply by drawing on easily available sources, e.g. the street trader buying more apples from a wholesaler or farmer. **Long-term supply** allows for major changes in resources or technology, e.g. planting new orchards.

Supply schedule This is a table showing how much supply there is of a good or service at different price levels (usually short-term supply).

Supply curve This is a graphical representation of a supply schedule, where price is plotted on the vertical axis and quantity supplied is plotted on the horizontal axis.

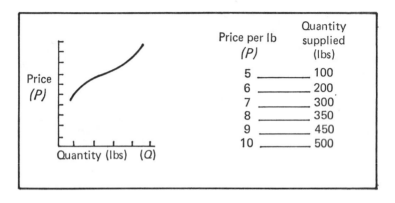

Price per lb (P)	Quantity supplied (lbs)
5	100
6	200
7	300
8	350
9	450
10	500

All short-term supply schedules and curves assume:
1 Costs of production, including wages, will not vary outside known limits.
2 Technology remains the same.
3 The number and capacity of potential suppliers remains the same.
4 Taxes or subsidies relating to the good or service will remain the same.

In other words, a supply schedule or curve shows how supply would react to a change in price only; all other possible variables affecting the selling situation are assumed to be unchanged.

'Normal' supply The supply of most commodities is determined by the costs of production. If the selling price of the commodity goes up, less efficient producers will be able to enter the market and therefore the quantity supplied will increase. This is shown on the supply curve by a curve sloping upward from left to right.

Extension of supply An increase in quantity supplied resulting from a change in price is shown as a movement *along* a supply curve.

Contraction of supply A decrease in the quantity supplied resulting from a change in price is also shown as a movement *along* a supply curve.

Shift in supply If any of the basic assumptions on which the supply schedule/curve rests are altered, then a *new* curve is drawn: for example if raw material prices increase, producers may offer less for sale at all price levels.

Elasticity of supply

This is a measure of the extent to which the quantity supplied varies when another factor affecting supply varies. For O level study it is usual to consider only **price elasticity of supply**, i.e. a measure of the extent to which the supply of a commodity varies when price varies. It is calculated by the formula:

$$\frac{\% \text{ change in quantity supplied}}{\% \text{ change in price}}$$

Elasticity and inelasticity of supply are measured and interpreted in the same way as for demand.

Practical uses of price elasticity of supply

1 Manufacturers who buy components from several small suppliers will want to estimate how much they need to offer these suppliers if they want to increase production.
2 If the government offers a subsidy to producers it will need to know the change in supply which will result.

Factors determining elasticity of supply

1 The extent to which capital and other resources are being used. If there is spare productive capacity, output may be easily increased in response to a price increase.
2 The availability of all the resources needed in the production of a commodity. For instance if there is a shortage of cocoa the supply of chocolate will be limited, regardless of changes in price.
3 The type of equipment required in production, e.g. ten years may be needed to build a new electricity power station in response to an increase in price, but ten days might be sufficient to switch production from skirts to blouses.

Here is a sample question on supply:

1 What does the economist mean by supply? What factors influence the supply of any commodity? (WEL) (Amended)

Equilibrium price

This is the price in a market; i.e. when buyers and sellers come together, where the quantity demanded is equal to the quantity supplied. This can be represented diagrammatically by a simple cross showing the inter- section of demand and supply. At price P consumers demand quantity Q

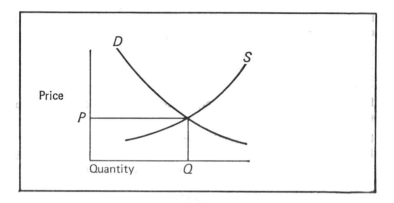

and the industry is prepared to supply the same amount. If the price is above P, there will be an excess of supply and sellers will be left with unsold goods. If the price is below P, buyers will not be able to get all they want. If there is a shift in demand or a shift in supply, then new conditions will be in force and a new equilibrium price will come about.

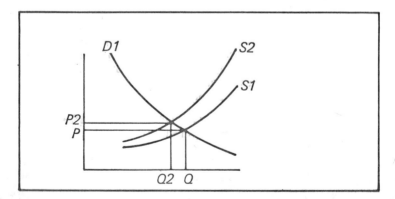

In the second figure there is a new equilibrium price P_2 and a new equilibrium quantity Q_2, the result of a shift in supply, caused for example by an increase in wage costs.

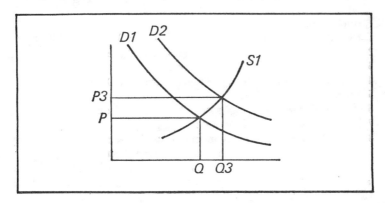

In the third figure the new equilibrium points, P_3 and Q_3, are the results of shift in demand, caused, for example, by an increase in incomes of buyers.

You should be familiar with this kind of diagram because essay questions often ask you to reproduce such a graph.

2 *Explain with the aid of diagrams the theoretical effects on the market price of new cars of*
   (a) *decrease in the price of petrol*
   (b) *restriction on imported cars*
   (c) *increase in investment by companies producing cars.* (JMB)

The market

Market means the coming together of buyers and sellers. **Market demand** means the total demand effect of all individual buyers combined together. It is usually assumed for O level studies that buyers behave independently of each other and each buyer is unable to affect the determination of market price. **Market supply** means the total supply effect of all individual producers combined together. It cannot be assumed that suppliers are always unable to affect price: for instance, of the many situations one sometimes studies at O level consider the case of monopoly.

Monopoly

A monopoly situation is when a single firm by regulating supply can determine the price of a commodity, e.g. Iran by reducing the amount of oil it will supply increases world price of oil.

A monopoly position can be achieved by:

1 **Product differentiation**, e.g. Kellogg's corn flakes, Panadol
2 **Goodwill** – a firm's reputation, e.g. Ribena, Vaseline
3 **Conditions of supply**, e.g. oil, bread
4 **Horizontal integration**, e.g. Rank Hovis McDougall
5 **Patents**, e.g. cats' eyes
6 **Acts of Parliament**, e.g. post and telecommunications
7 **Natural monopolies**, e.g. water
8 **Cartels** – this is not really monopoly but an arrangement whereby firms combine together to create the same effect.

Monopolies are distrusted because they can result in high prices, and lack of competition often adversely affects quality, service and research and development.

Monopolies can be economically advantageous if they are supervised so as to ensure that the consumer is not exploited:

1 Economies of scale can result
2 Wasteful competition is eliminated
3 Excess capacity is avoided

3 *What is monopoly? Name any two industries that contain monopolies. What are the advantages and disadvantages of monopolies?* (OX)

Examination preparation

Objective test study material

Prepare definitions for the following

Utility   Extension and contraction of demand and supply   Shift in demand and supply   Elasticity of demand   Elasticity of supply Inferior good   Equilibrium price

Calculations

1 Be able to work out the price elasticity of demand and supply.
2 Calculate the shifts in demand and supply from changes in demand/supply conditions. For example, be able to determine the new supply curve caused by an imposition of a tax.

Diagrammatical material

You should be able to draw supply and demand curves from data provided and thus work out an equilibrium price as well as being able to show diagramatically a shift in either demand or supply curves and thus work out new equilibrium price.

Essay questions

A popular type of question is that which asks the results of a change in the conditions of demand or supply. For example,

What will be the effects on the market for cigarettes after a successful government anti-smoking campaign?

Points to note about this type of question:

1 The question should be approached diagramatically.
2 Start with the equilibrium position.
3 Superimpose on this diagram of equilibrium the shift in demand (supply) curve.
4 Move only the demand (supply) curve.
5 On the diagram mark new price and amount demanded (supplied).
6 In a paragraph explain the diagram and explain the shift.

Thus your answer may look like this:

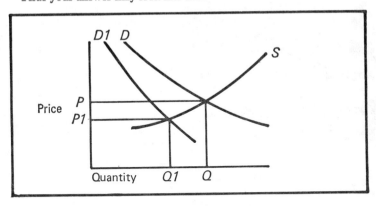

A successful anti-smoking campaign will reduce the demand for cigarettes at all price levels because buyers will drop out of the market. The demand curve will therefore shift to the left. The conditions of supply will be unchanged. The new equilibrium price will be P_1 reflecting a fall in price. The amount demanded will now be Q_1 showing a fall in the amount demanded.

The second type of question is usually of a more general nature.

Distinguish between an extension of demand and an increase in demand. What will be the effects of a marked increase in the price of petrol?

Para 1 Explain that **extension of demand** is a movement down a demand curve caused by a fall in price, i.e. from P to P_1.

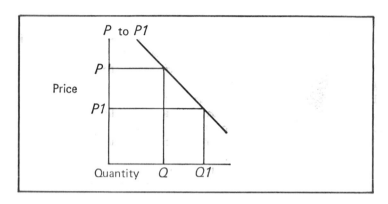

Thus, Q to Q_1 reflects an extension.

Para 2 Explain that **shift in demand** is an increase in demand at every price level.

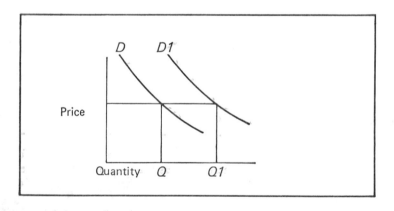

The movement from D to D_1 represents an increase in demand. At price P the amount demanded increases from Q to Q_1.

The second half of this question is more general. It is seeking an understanding and awareness of the practical effects of changes in market conditions. These are the types of points to include:

Para 3 The most obvious point to mention is that there will be a fall in demand for petrol with consequent effects on garages and commuters as motorists will buy less petrol. Refer to inelastic nature of the demand for petrol; thus price increase needs to be substantial for this to occur.

Para 4 Mention that there should be a drop in demand for cars or at least a shift to smaller cars. Point out the effects of this on employment directly and indirectly (**subsidiary industries**). The roles of advertising, motor bikes (as imports) and bicycles should also be raised in your answer.

Para 5 There will be an increase in the demand for public transport. Point out the effects of this on employment, road traffic, etc. Discuss how this might affect government policy on investment etc.

Para 6 You could mention the effects on the tourism industry. For instance the number of day trips may be reduced. Also mention the effect on air fares, hotels, etc.

Possible marking scheme
The first half of this question is worth 8 marks, 4 marks each for para 1 and para 2. The nature of the second half of the question necessitates a rather imprecise marking scheme. The general rule will be 1 mark for mentioning an effect, then up to 3 more marks for a full development. Thus, perhaps 3 or 4 points for development are being looked for, making the second half of the question worth a maximum of 12 marks.

Examination practice

4 *Explain the terms 'supply' and 'demand'. What are the main factors affecting*
  (a) *supply of wool*
  (b) *demand for wool?* (OX)
5 (a) *What conditions are necessary for a monopolist to exist?*
  (b) *What are the advantages and disadvantages of a monopoly?* (RSA)
6 (a) *With reference to price elasticity and with the use of diagrams explain (i) elastic demand (ii) inelastic demand.*
  (b) *What factors determine the elasticity of demand?* (RSA)
7 (a) *With the use of diagrams, explain the meaning of:*

      (*i*) *a shift in the demand curve*
     (*ii*) *a shift in the supply curve.*
  (*b*) *Give a full account of the factors which cause such shifts.* (RSA)

11 Money and banking

Synopsis A modern developed economy cannot operate without an efficient monetary system. The functions of money and the main types of money must be known. Knowledge about the working of the banking system and the special role of the Bank of England is very important.

*

Money

Money is sometimes defined as 'money is what money does', i.e. anything which fulfils the functions of money is money.

Functions of money
1 To act as a **medium of exchange**, i.e. to make possible an **exchange economy** where the **division of labour** may be used to a very great extent.
2 To act as a **standard of value**, again making an exchange system work more easily.
3 To act as a **store of value**, thus making it possible to make exchanges in two distinct stages in contrast to **barter** where the exchange of two commodities usually occurs simultaneously.
4 To make possible **deferred payments** by the use of an accounting system which allows for transactions on credit.

Desirable qualities of money
1 **Acceptability** People have confidence in it and are prepared to use it.
2 **Scarcity** The total supply must be strictly controlled to protect its value.

3 **Portability** Currency must be easy to handle.

4 **Durability** Currency must have a reasonable life.

5 **Divisibility** Currency must be capable of being used for large and small transactions.

6 **Uniformity** This helps to increase acceptability.

The most important of these qualities is acceptability. Although in certain circumstances individuals are quite happy to use plastic tokens, postage stamps, trading stamps etc., as money, the form of money that is generally acceptable is that issued by the government. All governments define a particular form of money – **legal tender**. This is the form in which a national currency appears, which must be used for official transactions, e.g. paying taxes, and which must be accepted in payments of debts between individuals.

Types of money

Coins Coins are made by the **Royal Mint** and introduced into circulation through the **Bank of England**. They are very important to ordinary members of the public for everyday transactions, but they represent a very small part of the total money supply.

Notes Bank notes are issued by the Bank of England, the only bank allowed to do so in England, and by some Scottish and Northern Irish banks. There are some special restrictions about note issue, but the main factor determining the quantity of notes in circulation is the need of the public for ready cash. In 1978 the average total of notes in circulation was about £9000m.

Bank money The most important form of money in the UK is that held in the form of bank deposits.

Cheques Strictly speaking, cheques are not money in themselves but the key to money, i.e. a cheque is an instruction to a bank from a customer telling the bank to pay money out of his bank account. Although not legal tender, cheques do fulfil the functions of money for many people, especially when used with a cheque card which gives the cheque increased acceptability.

Credit cards These too are related to bank accounts, but when they are used they are acting as money, fulfilling the function of a medium of exchange.

Note It is important to understand the distinction between **cash,** meaning notes and coins, and **money,** meaning all forms of money including legal tender, notes and coins up to the prescribed limit, and all other common ways of helping to make exchange possible apart from direct barter. Thus it is possible to imagine a developed economy which is cashless, but only a very simple economy, with limited exchange, which can exist without money.

1 Money is a medium of exchange, a measure, a standard and a measure of value. Discuss. (LOND)
2 What are the main forms of money used in the UK today? How can commercial banks 'create' money? (AEB)

Banking

Functions of banks

Banks are businesses, usually public joint stock companies, whose primary function is to make profits for their shareholders by carrying out banking activities.

Types of bank

High street banks These are sometimes known as **joint stock banks, clearing house banks, commercial banks** or **primary banks**. The most important are the **Big Four**, Barclays, Lloyds, Midland and National Westminster, which together carry out over 90 per cent of banking business.

Secondary banks These are specialist firms which concentrate on certain aspects of banking, e.g. providing funds for industry and commerce, rather than covering the whole range of banking activities. There are over 600 of them, but many are very small, compared to the high street banks.

The Bank of England This is the **central bank** of the UK and was nationalized in 1946.

Functions of commercial banks

(At O level it is sufficient to deal only with the functions of high street banks.)

1 Accept deposits of money through
   (a) **Current** (**cheque**) accounts
   (b) **Deposit** (**time**) accounts.
2 Keep deposits safe but readily available to customers by means of a cheque system, **standing orders** and other systems of transferring money.
3 Make various kinds of loans
   (a) **advances** usually a fixed sum for a fixed period
   (b) **overdraft** the right to issue cheques, up to an agreed amount, when current account funds are exhausted

(c) **money at call** very short-term loans to other banks or institutions in the **money market**.

Bank loans differ from loans between private individuals because a private loan is merely a temporary transfer of purchasing power, from lender to borrower, whereas a bank loan *creates* money, by giving credit to the borrower, without reducing the purchasing power of the lender. Because of this special power, banks need to exercise self-control and to be subject to outside control.

3 What are the main functions of commercial banks? (OX)

Banking 'rules'
Certain unwritten rules exist in banking. Banks depend on the confidence of their customers. To do this, they must have enough **liquid assets**, i.e. those easily converted into cash, to meet all anticipated demands by customers. However, liquid assets are not very profitable and bank shareholders want profits. Good banking involves balancing these opposing forces of liquidity and profitability.

Written or formal rules
1 Banks must keep some of their assets (equivalent to at least 12½ per cent of certain **liabilities**) in an approved form. This is called the **eligible reserve asset ratio**.
2 These eligible reserve assets are, broadly speaking, the most liquid (easily converted into cash) assets. The most important exception is that cash itself (money kept in the till at a bank) is not counted as an eligible reserve asset.
3 Each bank must keep a daily balance, equal to at least 1½ per cent of assets, in an account at the Bank of England.
4 Banks must make **special deposits** with the Bank of England when required. These special deposits are not eligible reserve assets.
5 These rules apply to primary banks but there are rules applying to secondary banks, which have the same restrictive effects.

Services provided by banks
As well as carrying out basic banking functions, banks offer a wide variety of other services in order to attract new customers or to keep existing customers.

Basic banking services These include the following: cheque books, cheque cards, credit cards, cash cards, standing orders, banker's order, direct debit, foreign exchange, travellers' cheques, night safes, and loans.
Bank services using special facilities and expertise These include

safe deposits, stockbroking, business contacts, providing references, foreign trade information, and acting as trustees and executors.

Bank services to attract customers
These include home safes, student accounts, economic data and other publications.

Role of the Bank of England
The government's bank
1 Manages the government's account.
2 Manages sales of Treasury bills, the **national debt** and government stock.
3 Carries out government **monetary policy** through the **money supply**.
4 Maintains the external value of the pound (when a fixed exchange system is in force or through intervention in foreign exchange markets at other times).
5 Acts as adviser and agent for the government in financial matters at home and abroad.

The banker's bank
1 Provides **clearing house** facilities.
2 Lends, in the last resort, to the high street banks.
3 Acts as leader of the banking community.

Powers of the Bank of England
1 **Special deposits** This is a means of affecting the quantity of the banks' reserve assets and therefore their ability to create credit.
2 **Directives** These are specific limitations on the type or quantity of bank lending.
3 **Open market operations** Through these the Bank is able to work on the level of deposits held in banks and therefore the ability to create credit.
4 **Minimum lending rate** The Bank sets this rate as the minimum at which it will lend to the banks and this is instrumental in determining the banks' base rates which indirectly affect the demand for bank loans.
5 **Persuasion** i.e. using the respect that has been built up in its long history. Although this sounds the weakest power, the banking system knows that if it does not accept Bank of England advice, then a more formal, rigorous set of rules may be imposed.

4 *The Bank of England's main function is the control of money.*
Comment. (LOND)

Examination preparation

Although questions are rarely set at O level on the way in which banks create credit, students are expected to have an understanding of the principles involved. These are

1 When customers deposit money in a bank the money still belongs to the customer but changes its form into bank money (a **book entry**).
2 Banking depends on the assumption that all customers will not want to draw all their money out, in the form of cash, at the same time.
3 It follows that as long as banks hold enough liquid assets to meet the needs of all their customers they will be safe. (Note the importance of customer confidence to the bank.)
4 Banks are able to make loans to customers, not by lending other customers' money, nor by lending shareholders' money, but by offering credit, i.e. opening bank accounts, which may be drawn upon in the usual way, so long as the total money in customers' accounts, those based on loans and those based on cash deposits, is not greater than the liquid assets available can support.
5 Because banks work on percentages when calculating the amount of liquid assets needed, it follows that if the bank receives an extra amount of liquid assets, this will make possible an increase in bank lending much greater than the original increase in liquid assets.
6 This multiplied effect, of increased cash deposits leading to greatly increased bank loans, works for the banking system as a whole and not just for the bank receiving the increased cash. For example, working on 10 per cent cash ratio, a bank receiving an extra £50 in cash will immediately be able to increase its loans by £45. This £45 if deposited in a bank will make possible another loan of £40.5. Eventually, if all money keeps returning to the banking system, all the banks together will be able to increase lending up to a maximum of £400.

Objective test study material
Many objective questions depend on an understanding of the balance sheet of a bank, what the various items mean and how they relate to one another.

Simplified balance sheet of a clearing house bank

Liabilities		Assets	
Deposits		Cash in till	100
Current accounts	5000	Balance at the Bank of England	150
Deposit accounts	5000	Special deposits	–
		Money at call	650
		Treasury bills	250
		Commercial bills	200
		Investments	2650
		Advances	6000
	10,000		10,000

Liabilities Claims on a business. If the business were to crease trading today, who would be entitled to receive part of whatever was left? In this case, customers have left £10,000 with the bank, half in current (cheque) accounts, half in deposit (time) accounts. Liabilities are a form of debt: it is money owed to another.

Assets What the business is worth. They always total the same as liabilities because they are two ways of looking at the same thing. The asset side answers the question, how much is the business worth today? The important aspect of the asset side of this balance sheet is the way in which assets are distributed under the different headings.

Cash in till The amount of ready cash kept available to meet the day-to-day needs of customers.

Balance at the Bank of England The bank's equivalent of its customers' current accounts. It is the easiest way banks can settle debts with each other. Each clearing bank must keep $1\frac{1}{2}$ per cent of its assets in this form.

Special deposits One way in which the Bank of England can quickly reduce the liquid assets of a bank and thereby reduce its ability to make loans. The Bank of England simply requires the banks to place some of their liabilities on deposit at the Bank so they are no longer eligible for lending against. Special deposits are not eligible for reserve assets.

Money at call A special form of short-term lending from banks to discount houses or to other banks.

Treasury bills A way used by the government to raise short-term (three months) loans.

Commercial bills These are a means of getting over a cash-flow problem in a business, e.g. a manufacturer selling goods to a retailer must give the retailer time to pay but may need cash himself before the retailer is due to pay him. The retailer's bill (promise to pay in three months) may be sold to a bill broker who may in turn sell it to a bank.

Investments This means holdings of stocks and shares, usually ones where there is very little risk involved.

Advances Loans to customers, either fixed amounts for a fixed period or overdrafts.

5 *List the main assets of a commercial bank. Explain what is meant by the eligible reserve asset ratio. What are special deposits? When are they used?* (JMB)

Diagrammatical material
It is unusual to find this part of the syllabus represented by this type of question at O level, but simple tables showing changes in the money supply or showing lending by different financial institutions may be set.

Essay questions
In many ways the essay questions on banking are the easiest in that they are invariably descriptive; that is, the questions simply require you to repeat acquired knowledge. The major problem is what material to select because in questions of this sort where the essays are rather wide it is impossible to include all the available knowledge in the space of half an hour.

Describe the major functions of the Bank of England.

It is important to note the title of the essay. A description of the main functions is needed and not simply a detailed description of *one* function. Also remember that when asked to describe the main functions obviously great detail is not required. Avoid the temptation to write at length. Mentioning the following points might be expected to obtain the maximum marks.

Para 1 Control of the money supply. You could expand this function by listing the means the Bank has: open market operations, special deposits, directives, minimum lending rate.

Para 2 The banker's bank. Here you should describe the clearing house operation and settlement of debts. Also refer to the asset structure of the banks.

Para 3 Management of public sector debt. Define the debt and differentiate between short-term and long-term funding. Discuss the issue and redemption of stock and the problems involved with the payment of interest.

Para 4 Central government's bank. Mention the working of the Consolidated Fund and the Bank's role as adviser to the government and its control of the note issue.

Para 5 Responsibility for external value of pound and matters concerning foreign currency. Refer to the working of the exchange equalization account, exchange control and the fact that the Bank holds all foreign reserves.

Possible marking scheme

In such a question a detailed marking scheme is impossible to draft because the material is so wide-ranging. The examiner in awarding 20 marks will probably be looking for five functions to be named and described. The normal procedure is therefore to award 1 mark for mentioning a function and up to 3 marks for expanding each function. Any candidate writing on one function, say paragraph 1, control of the money supply, will therefore limit his total marks to 4.

What are the major functions of a joint stock bank?

Again the major problem facing candidates is in the selection of material. One way of answering this question is to look for broad groups of functions, perhaps five. Thus, the following outline would obtain high marks.

Para 1 Accepting deposits. Distinguish between current and deposit accounts.

Para 2 Lending money. Discuss the different ways: loans, overdrafts, credit cards, budget accounts.

Para 3 Providing methods of payment. Your list should inlcude cheques, standing orders, direct debits and credit transfers.

Para 4 Aids to business. Examples you could raise include night safes, bankers' drafts, overseas sales, tax advice.

Para 5 Customer services. Include travellers' cheques, trustees, cash dispensers and cheque cards in your answer.

Possible marking scheme

With five broad groups of functions the maximum marks under each heading is 4 regardless of the depth of development.

Just as candidates must select material to include, examiners must agree on the awarding of marks. Because the above type of marking scheme is fairly tight examiners often adopt the method of merely looking for a list of functions. They then award 1 mark for mentioning a function and an additional mark may be awarded for expansion. Perhaps an additional 2 marks may be given for expanding the more important functions such as bank loans and overdrafts. This approach is very fair and because the functions far exceed ten in number candidates who are well prepared can easily obtain high marks.

Examination practice

6 *To facilitate trade any form of society needs money. Why?* (JMB)
7 *Describe the process of credit creation. For what reasons may the central bank aim to regulate the creation of credit?* (LOND)
8 *Give an account of the functions of the central bank.* (RSA)

12 Inflation

Synopsis Inflation has become an increasingly important feature of the UK economy, so it is only to be expected that examination papers will usually include a question on inflation.

It is not a problem to which there are easy solutions. Students must be aware of the ways of measuring inflation (with their limitations), the possible causes and the possible cures (with some understanding of what considerable results may follow).

*

Definition of inflation

Inflation in everyday usage means 'blowing up' as applied to balloons. In economics it relates specifically to the general price level and is simply a situation where prices are increasing. Sometimes the definition of 'too much money chasing too few goods' is used, but this is too narrow for general use because it describes only one inflationary situation.

Measurement of inflation

In most economies, it is normal for the prices of many goods or services to vary throughout a year. The price of fruit and vegetables varies according to the season (e.g. strawberries). New products introduced to a market sometimes start life highly priced and gradually become cheaper.

In some circumstances the ordinary consumer becomes aware that although some prices are going down, most prices are going up, but by different degrees. Money does not go as far as it did. Economists try to quantify this general feeling of price increase by using index numbers as measures of change. The mechanics of index numbers will be considered later in this chapter, but at this stage it is important to stress that index numbers are only averages and cannot be used as precise measures of the extent of price changes for all producers and consumers in an economy.

Causes of inflation

It is usual to identify two distinct possible causes of inflation, **demand pull** and **cost push**.

'Demand pull' describes the situation where the purchasing power, i.e. money available for spending (sometimes called **aggregate demand**), rises faster than the available supply of goods and services on which to spend money. This may happen because:

1 Incomes from work have increased beyond the increase in **productivity**.
2 State benefits – child allowances, pensions etc. – have increased more than the level of government income (such as taxation) collected for this purpose.
3 Credit has expanded – i.e. more spending of borrowed money, such as hire purchase or bank loans, is taking place, possibly because easier terms or lower interest rates are available.
4 Government expenditure on hospitals, roads, schools etc. may have increased beyond the level of government income (this is called deficit budgeting).

It must be noted that any of these causes may have a **multiplier effect,** far greater than the original increase in purchasing power, as additional expenditure becomes additional income to someone else and so leads to more expenditure starting a chain reaction.

The result of an increase in purchasing power greater than the available supply of goods and services means that sellers, faced with more would-be buyers than they can satisfy, raise prices so that, in effect, buyers are bidding against each other. This is what happens every year when the number of people wishing to attend the FA Cup Final is far greater than the available number of tickets and so cup final tickets fetch very high prices.

'Cost push' describes the situation where costs of production increase and this increase to the producers is passed on to the consumer in higher prices. This may happen because

1 Wages increase faster than productivity.

2 Basic materials increase in price. Thus an increase in the price of oil or of coal will trigger off price increases in many other goods and services in whose production they are used.

3 A reduction in the amount of work done, either because of shorter hours or longer holidays, with no reduction in wages paid, means lower output for the same cost.

4 Inadequate investment in plant and equipment may reduce productivity.

'Cost push' is often accepted by consumers as a justification for price increases, whereas 'demand pull' is often thought to be unfair. However 'cost push' need not inevitably lead to higher prices: it could lead to development of substitute materials, greater use of technological developments and greater efficiency. Sometimes it may be used as an excuse for increasing prices beyond the actual increase in costs.

The division between 'demand pull' and 'cost push' inflation is not rigid; often the factors causing one or other may interact. The best example is the 'inflationary spiral' or 'wage–price spiral'. Increased food prices may lead to increased wage demands which if met result in 'demand pull' inflation. These increased wages may be passed on to consumers in higher prices (cost push inflation).

The effects of inflation

Inflation will not affect all producers and consumers in the same way nor will the same effects always be felt by individuals. For instance, people whose incomes rise faster than the rate of inflation will not suffer any reduction in their standard of living. Producers will react differently to **'creeping inflation'** of about 2 or 3 per cent per year than to **'galloping inflation'** of 30 per cent per year. It is necessary, therefore, to consider a few inflationary situations and deduce the effects on some of the people involved.

1 If the rate of inflation exceeds the rate of foreign competitors, then exports may fall (because of uncompetitive prices) and imports may rise (because they are more competitively priced). This may lead to a devaluation of the currency.

2 If the rate of inflation is high, businesses may lose confidence (profitability of future business becomes very difficult to estimate) and there may be a fall in investment. A fall in investment may also result from a reduction in the amount of saving possible. Reduced investment could lead to increased unemployment.

3 If the rate of inflation is higher than the rate of interest on borrowed money, it becomes sensible to borrow in order to buy now before prices rise. This would result in increased demand and possibly further 'demand pull' inflation.

4 In any inflationary situation, those on **fixed incomes** suffer in 'real' terms, i.e. they can buy less with their money. This applies to people such as pensioners when pension increases lag behind price increases.

5 Workers belonging to trade unions with weak bargaining powers, or those in an industry with no union, tend to obtain smaller increases than other workers and thus the gap between high and low earnings widens (e.g. shop assistants and farm-workers).

6 Direct taxes, which are designed to be progressive, sometimes hit hardest the people they are designed to help, if allowances and tax bands are not altered in line with the inflation rate. This is a major cause of the **poverty trap** which means that people on low incomes become worse off in real terms through loss of income-related benefit, as their income rises.

7 Borrowers, especially long-term, benefit from a period of inflation. House purchasers are not put off by high mortgage rates, knowing that as years pass the 'burden' of repayments will become easier as their incomes increase, thus there is a tendency for house prices to rise rapidly.

Here is an example of the kind of general question you may expect to see on inflation.

1 What are the causes of inflation? Discuss its possible effects. (JMB)

Cures for inflation

If inflation is caused by excess demand and/or increased costs, then the cure for inflation must theoretically involve curbing demand and/or keeping costs down. In reality the cure for inflation is not simple, as recent experience in the UK shows, and all remedies must be presented with qualifications and with caution. The government may try some of the following policies:

Reduce demand

The following are some of the common government policies aimed at reducing demand:

1 Introduce a wages policy to keep down the extent of wage increases. This may be statutory (compulsory with legal backing) or voluntary (trade unions persuaded by government to accept restrictions).

Experience suggests that either sort of policy needs general acceptance by the public (including the trade unions) and works only for a limited time.

2 The government may reduce the amount of money in the economy by applying monetary policies on the banking system. Such measures may include open market operations, changes in MLR, special deposits and directives (see Chapter 11 on 'Money and Banking'). In reducing the amount of money in the economy, especially by limiting bank lending, the effect may well be to hit hardest businesses which cannot expand and may even go out of existence, increase unemployment and reduce economic activity.

3 It may change its **fiscal policies**; use taxation, to reduce the purchasing power in the economy, for instance by increasing the rate of income tax. However, this may lead to further pressures for wage increases leading to further cost push inflation.

4 The government may attempt to reduce spending by tightening hire purchase and other forms of credit buying. This will be unpopular with both producers and consumers and democratically elected governments are limited in the amount of unpopularity they can withstand.

5 It may reduce its own expenditure. This may be capital expenditure on new schools, hospitals, roads etc. or current expenditure on the wages of those who provide public services. Either way it would result in reduced standards of public services and/or in higher unemployment.

Control costs of production

1 Use a wages policy to limit wage increases (with the limitations already indicated).

2 Introduce a system of **subsidies** to keep prices and costs of production down, e.g. a grant to the NCB to keep coal prices and hence electricity prices down. Subsidies are always very expensive to operate and may distort market forces and encourage inefficiency.

3 Use a body such as the **Price Commission** to check the fairness of price increases. Such a body may have no powers to prevent increases (especially over imported basic materials) and may be slow in dealing with all cases.

2 What are the main causes of inflation? How has the government attempted to overcome inflation in recent years? (OX)

Index numbers

There are many different ways of measuring price changes, each one stressing different variables – wholesale prices, leading firms, capital goods, consumer goods etc. The most widely known and used is the **index of retail prices**, compiled by the Department of Employment and often called 'the cost of living index'. It is calculated as follows:

1 A list of items showing the goods and services on which an average family spends its money is assembled.

2 **Weights**, showing the relative importance of the various items, are given. The weights are related to weekly expenditure on each item, the greater the expenditure, the greater the weight.

3 A **base** time (year/period) is chosen which becomes the standard against which price changes are measured. This is given the number 100.

4 Price increases for each item (averaged from sample findings) are expressed as per cent increases and multiplied by the correct weight.

5 The new total of price changes times weight for each item is divided by the total of the weights.

6 The resultant figure is compared to the 100 of the base year.

The weaknesses of using the retail prices index as a measure of inflation are:

1 Weighting reflects the original importance of items and takes no account of changing popularity or unpopularity.

2 Regional variations exist in food prices, housing prices, transport costs etc. These all become blurred in a single average.

3 A single figure does not indicate which prices are rising faster than others.

4 The choice of the base year may distort the picture (a year of very high prices or very low prices)

3 *How can the rate of inflation be measured? What are the problems involved in the measurement of inflation?* (OX)

Examination preparation

Objective test study material

Prepare definitions for the following

Inflation Cost push Demand pull Creeping inflation Galloping inflation Aggregate demand Productivity Investment Poverty trap Monetary policy Fiscal policy Public sector expenditure

Factual information You may be asked to identify correct policies for given situations, possible effects of inflation gainers/losers from particular situations and causes of inflation.

Calculations You should be able to perform simple manipulation of index number data.

Index numbers

Items	Weekly expenditure year 1 (base)	Weight	Weight × expenditure
Food and drink	20	40	800
Housing	10	20	200
Entertainment	5	10	50
Other	15	30	450
		100	1500 = Index Value 100

	Weekly expenditure year 2	% change from year 1	Weight	Weight × % change
Food and drink	30	+50	40	+2000
Housing	20	+100	20	+2000
Entertainment	10	+100	10	+1000
Other	10	−33⅓	30	−1000
				4000

4000 ÷ 100 (sum of weights) = 40
Index for year 2 = 100 + 40 = 140.

Diagrammatical material
Information about inflation over a period of time for one or more countries may be presented in charts or tables and interpretation called for.

Supply and demand curves may be used to illustrate 'cost push' and 'demand pull' inflation as follows overleaf:

Cost push

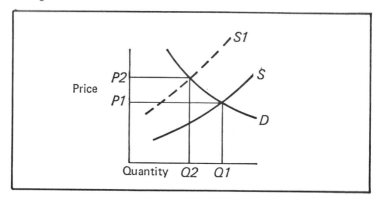

S_1 represents a shift in supply as new supply conditions (increased labour, raw materials and other costs) now apply. Note that demand remains unchanged.

Demand pull

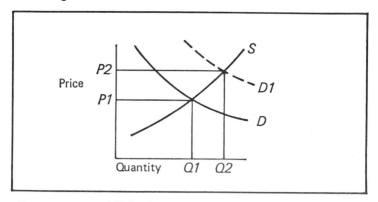

D_1 represents a shift in demand as new demand conditions (greater income) apply. Note that supply remains unchanged.

Essay questions

It is always crucial to answer questions directly and this applies especially to questions about inflation. If the question asks about the effects of inflation then no marks will be awarded for listing the causes. Read and digest the question very carefully. Do not be dogmatic in your statements: 'possible', 'probable', 'maybe' should be found throughout your answer.

To what extent can inflation be cured by a government incomes policy?

Para 1 Define inflation. Outline briefly demand pull and cost push and mention that they are often inter-related.

Para 2 Point out that to curb inflation it is necessary either to reduce demand or to reduce (or keep constant) costs. The idea of an incomes policy is to attempt both of these aims. Explain how this is done.

Para 3 It is doubtful if incomes policies will be successful because of (a) difficulties in achieving such a policy (explain the difference between voluntary and statutory); (b) a need for policy to be operated with other policies, e.g. investment; and (c) success may depend on external factors.

Para 4 Britain depends on imports, especially raw materials and food. If world prices rise (e.g. poor harvests, oil) this is immediately reflected in internal price rises.

Para 5 A successful incomes policy must be accompanied by a reduction in public expenditure. Explain why. This is difficult to achieve. Explain why.

Para 6 To combat inflation the money supply must be reduced. Explain why and describe the appropriate tax policies. Explain the difficulties.

Para 7 Further measures to control the money supply include reduction of credit. Explain why and how this is done.

Para 8 Refer to the long-term problems: (a) ending of incomes policy, followed by wage explosions; (b) real cause may be outdated and inefficient methods of production; (c) increased unemployment may result from decreasing demand; (d) how long can unpopular policies be carried out in a free democracy?

Possible marking scheme

Para 1   2 marks for definition, 2 marks for extension.

Para 2   2 marks for aims of incomes policy, 2 for explanation.

Para 3   (a) 1 mark (b) 1 mark (c) 1 mark.

Para 4   Effects of dependence on imports: 2 marks; example: 1 mark.

Para 5   Need for reduction in public expenditure: 1 mark.
         Reasons: 1 mark; reasons for difficulty in achieving: 1 mark.

Para 6   Need for reduction in money supply: 1 mark; reason: 1 mark; tax policies: 1 mark.

Para 7   Need for reduction in credit: 1 mark; reason: 1 mark.

Para 8   (a) 1 mark (b) 1 mark (c) 1 mark (d) 1 mark.

Note these marks total 26 but the maximum available will be 20. The danger to avoid is in concentrating on a few points and writing at length rather than presenting the full picture in a brief form, keeping within the constraints of limited examination time.

Examination practice

4 *For each type of inflation discuss the economic policies a government might introduce to bring down the rate of inflation.* (RSA)
5 (a) *Define the term 'inflation'.*
  (b) *What are the effects of inflation?* (RSA)

13   Public finance

Synopsis In a mixed economy such as the UK, the government is a major producer and consumer. It also controls many aspects of the private sector. Much of this control depends on the way in which the government gets its income and on how it spends it.

*

Objects of government expenditure

Public expenditure refers to the spending of the central government, local authorities and public corporations. The amount of public expenditure is approximately equivalent to half the country's production. In money terms this amounted to £76,000m in 1978, but figures are both constantly changing and difficult to comprehend.

Approximately 60 per cent of the total expenditure is spent by central government and local authorities on goods and services. This amount is distributed between social services (education, health, social security benefits), local and environmental services (housing, roads, law and order), defence and foreign relations and expenditure by public corporations – new power stations, steel mills etc.

The other 40 per cent of expenditure is paid in grants, subsidies and interest payments on national savings and government bonds (repayment of the **national debt**).

The size of this expenditure, accounting for 35 per cent of all spending on goods and services, makes it very important in the management of the economy, hence the recent emphasis on public expenditure by successive governments. It is generally accepted that

1 An increase in public expenditure can affect the rate of inflation (demand pull). A reduction can have deflationary effects.

2 An increase in public expenditure can reduce unemployment and perhaps cause a shortage of labour. A decrease in public expenditure can cause unemployment.

3 The pattern of expenditure is important, e.g. capital expenditure on motorways increases employment, capital spending on purchase of buildings housing government offices previously rented has no effect on employment levels. Certain industries can be encouraged or discouraged by government contracts and subsidies, e.g. building and construction.

4 An increase in public expenditure might involve an increase in the public sector borrowing requirement (PSBR) which has important inflationary effects. Such a high level of expenditure must relate to a high level of income. Governments have three options:

(a) A **balanced budget** means that government expenditure equals government income.

(b) A **deficit budget** means that government expenditure exceeds government income and thus borrowing is necessary. (This could be deliberate policy to encourage higher employment levels.)

(c) A **surplus budget** means that government income exceeds government expenditure; again this could be deliberate policy to take money out of the economy and thus reduce the rate of inflation.

The following is a sample question on public expenditure.

1 Outline the main items of expenditure by the central government. (WEL) (Amended)

Sources of government income

Direct taxes

Income tax This is a **proportional** and **progressive tax**. It is proportional in that assessment is made on a percentage basis and progressive in that the higher a person's income, the higher the proportion of that income is paid in tax. (*Note* The higher income earner does not simply pay more tax than a lower income earner; he pays *proportionately* more.) It is levied on individuals and on partnerships.

Corporation tax A percentage tax on a company's profits. It is a proportional tax because the firm is liable for the same percentage of tax on profits regardless of the amount of profits made. (This is now a two-tier tax, but the basic principle remains the same.)

Capital gains tax A percentage tax on the disposal (sale) of capital – paintings, shares etc.

Capital transfer tax A tax on gifts made during the life or on the estate of a deceased person. This replaces estate duty (death duties).

Indirect taxes

All indirect taxes are **regressive** i.e. the lower income groups pay a higher proportion of their incomes in tax. Note they do not pay more, they simply pay a higher *percentage* of their income in tax than do the higher income groups. Indirect taxes include

Value Added Tax VAT is a tax imposed on all goods and services at all stages of their production process. A few basic goods such as food, children's clothes and shoes are exempt.

Excise duty A tax on alcohol, petrol, tobacco and other home produced goods.

Customs duty A tax on goods imported into the country.

Betting duties A tax on forms of gambling including horse racing and football pools.

Rates These are a tax levied by local authorities on property within the local authority areas. This is an independent source of revenue which supplements a grant to local authorities from central government. But because of increasing public expenditure it is a falling *proportion* of local authority income – despite recent substantial rises in the level of rates.

The government has sources of income other than taxes:

Trading surpluses This will include profits from public corporations, the income of water authorities and similar organizations, as well as rent from corporation houses.

National insurance contributions This is simply the income from the compulsory national insurance contributions from all workers in full-time or part-time employment or self-employment.

Motor vehicle and other licences As well as 'road tax', this category includes the fees for passports and licences for dogs and guns.

Borrowing The government borrows short-term, e.g. Treasury bills, and long-term, e.g. government stock (**gilts**). The amount the government needs to borrow annually is called the **public sector borrowing requirement** (PSBR). It totals about one-sixth of the amount raised by taxation and national insurance contributions. Accumulated government borrowing over the years forms the **national debt**.

The most important source of revenue is taxation. There is considerable debate on what forms this taxation should take. More specifically should the tax be a predominantly **direct taxation,** that is, on incomes, profits, dividends and acquired wealth, or should tax predominantly be **indirect taxation**, that is, tax on the sales of goods and services. There are arguments for and against both types of taxation:

Advantages of direct taxation

1 Socially just. Lower income earners pay no tax or a smaller proportion of their income in tax than higher income groups.
2 Provides a means of income redistribution. Money collected from the higher income groups can be distributed to poorer sections of the community in the form of various benefits – child allowances, family income supplement etc.
3 Can be regulated to assist government's economic policy. A reduction in taxation levels can generate increased expenditure in times of unemployment. Conversely, in periods of inflation, increased tax reduces aggregate demand.
4 The tax is not directly inflationary.
5 The tax is easy and relatively cheap to collect. The amount collected is easy to predict.

Disadvantages of direct taxation

1 Acts as a major disincentive to effort. Why work harder and longer if the increased wages and profits are heavily taxed?
2 Efficient firms suffer because when efficiency results in higher profits these are subject to a high level of taxation.
3 A consequence of the first two disadvantages is that investment might be adversely affected and/or result in investment going overseas.
4 High levels of taxation might reduce the level of foreign investment in Britain. It must be added that some believe this to be an advantage.
5 The higher income groups save a higher proportion of their income than lower income groups. If higher income groups are heavily taxed, then the level of savings will fall. This has wide-ranging economic effects, on investment, for example.
6 High levels of direct taxation result in tax avoidance. The figure at present is estimated at thousands of millions of pounds a year.

Advantages of indirect taxation

1 Income earners keep a higher proportion of their income at source. This acts as an incentive to hard work and effort from which there should be beneficial economic effects for society.

2 This allows an element of personal choice. Consumers know which goods are heavily taxed and thus can, in effect, decide whether to pay the tax by buying or not buying the goods in question.

3 The government has the ability to be selective. It can encourage or discourage certain industries by changing levels of taxation. This includes the ability to reduce the demand for goods which are imported.

4 It is an economic weapon with immediate effect. Thus, a reduction in the demand for oil can be achieved rapidly by an increase in tax on petrol.

Disadvantages of indirect taxation

1 Indirect taxes are regressive. The amount of tax on goods is fixed in money terms. Thus, lower income groups pay a higher proportion of their income in tax than do higher income groups.

2 An increase in indirect taxation has immediate inflationary effects by putting up the price of goods and services.

3 Indirect taxation can dislocate the market equilibrium by distorting supply conditions.

4 Indirect taxation creates a heavy burden of administrative and clerical work on both business and the civil service, e.g. VAT has proved expensive to collect and has proved particularly onerous to the small firms.

5 Firms in their early stages of development are unable to obtain tax relief; this might hamper their growth.

Here are two examples of essay questions about direct and indirect taxation.

2 (a) *What is the difference between direct and indirect taxes?*
    (b) *Trace the probable economic effects of each of the following*
        (i) *increase in income tax*
        (ii) *2 per cent reduction in VAT.* (RSA)

3 *What are the advantages and disadvantages for both government and taxpayer of*
    (a) *direct tax*
    (b) *indirect tax?* (OX)

Poverty trap

A large amount of government expenditure is aimed at reducing the effects of income inequality by giving help to those people who need it. The ways in which it does this include rate rebates, free school meals, clothing allowances, rent allowances, free prescriptions, family income supplement, etc. Many of these are **income-related benefits**: this means that only those whose income is below a certain level qualify for benefits. It can happen that an increase in earnings will place someone above the level which entitles him to benefit and yet the value of the benefits lost may be greater than the income increase, thus leaving the net income smaller. For example if a rise of £4 per week means losing £10 worth of benefits per week, the net loss is £6 per week. This acts as a disincentive to some people to increase their earnings.

This situation can arise because different government departments use different income scales for granting benefits and because the scales are not altered frequently enough to keep pace with inflation.

Examination preparation

Objective test study material
An important point about public finance is that although it does not lend itself to the essay type of question (it is one of the topics that is least used), it does allow a wide range of objective type questions. Therefore, you should be familiar with its terms.

Prepare definitions for the following
Public expenditure   Public sector borrowing   Balanced budget
Deficit budget   Surplus budget   Direct taxation   Indirect taxation
Progressive taxation   Regressive taxation   Percentage tax   Income redistribution
You should also be able to give examples of different types of tax.

Diagrammatical material
The various types of taxes may be shown diagrammatically and need to be recognized. Tables or bar charts might be given showing changing patterns of taxation or public expenditure. You might be asked to describe what is happening and suggest reasons for the shifts.

Essay questions
The types of essays are limited. They centre around the pattern of expenditure, the changing pattern of raising government revenue and the advantages and disadvantages of different types of taxation. For example,

Discuss the possible economic effects of a shift from direct to indirect forms of taxation.

This is a variation on the theme of the advantages and disadvantages of different types of taxation.

Para 1 Define and give examples of both direct and indirect taxes. State that any shift of emphasis would be gradual and therefore the effect would be gradual.

Para 2 Discuss how the two different forms affect personal incentive.

Para 3 Discuss how they affect investment, both from home and abroad.

Para 4 Talk about the effect a shift would have on the level of saving.

Para 5 Discuss the inflationary effects of a shift to indirect tax. Discuss the effects of this on wage claims.

Para 6 Point out that the lower income groups, especially pensioners, become economically worse off because of the regressive nature of indirect tax.

Para 7 Point out that indirect taxes are more expensive to collect.

Para 8 You could mention that with a shift to indirect taxes the government is given greater power to influence consumer behaviour.

Possible marking scheme
The first paragraph would be worth 4 marks. Any of the subsequent points made as illustration would be worth up to 4 marks – 1 mark for mentioning the effect, up to 3 marks for development.

Examination practice

4 *Outline the main direct and indirect taxes paid by a married man with three children earning £5000 a year.* (WEL)

5 *What is meant by the term 'national debt'? What would be the effects of a substantial reduction in government expenditure?* (AEB)

6 (a) *Choose one direct tax and one indirect tax and explain how each is levied.*

  (b) *Indicate the main advantages and disadvantages of each type of tax.* (RSA)

14   National income

Synopsis If a government assumes responsibility for controlling the economy, as all governments today do to some extent, it needs to have some way of measuring the success of its policies and to see where changes are necessary. National income accounting attempts to provide this kind of information. Students of economics need to know the principles on which national income calculations are based, the uses to which they are put and the special problems which arise.

*

The national income of a country is a measurement of the economic activity taking place there over a given period of time.

Gross national product This is the money value of all goods and services produced in a country in one year. It takes account of production by a country's nationals in other countries (such income would be mainly income from foreign assets), but does not make any allowance for using up capital resources.

Net national income The above figure after **depreciation,** i.e. the amount of the annual product which has to be used to replace used-up or worn-out capital, has been taken away from GNP.

Gross domestic product This is a measure of the value of the product produced within the country. It differs from GNP in that it omits income from abroad, unless received for exports.

Market price and factor cost These are two alternative ways of presenting national income figures. Market price means that output or expenditure is valued at the price the customer paid. Factor cost means that output or expenditure is valued at the price the producer receives. There will be a significant difference between the two approaches only if

indirect taxes or **subsidies** are significant, e.g. the difference between consumers' expenditure on, and producer's income from, whisky.

The circular flow

National income accounting, i.e. the calculation and presentation of a country's national income figures, is based on the concept of the circular flow. In its most simplified form, there are just two part to the economy, **producers** (industry) and **consumers** (the public). It is assumed, at first, that everything produced is consumed and that the economy is self-contained, i.e. there is no foreign trade. The diagrams show two ways of looking at the economic activity taking place. The left-hand

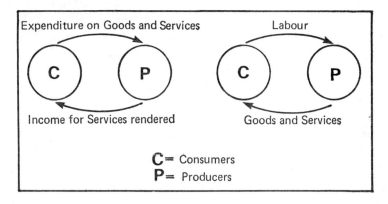

figure demonstrates how all income received by the public is a payment from industry (producers) for services provided by the public (consumers). In this diagram it also shows that all income is spent by the public on obtaining goods and services provided by industry. The right-hand figure shows that the goods and services are produced by industry with the help of economic activity by the public.

Measurement of the national income

Looking at the circular flow diagrams it is apparent that it is possible to measure the extent of economic activity in three ways. Firstly, the value of the output of goods and services can be totalled. Secondly, the expenditure on goods and services can be totalled. Thirdly, income received by the public for their economic activity can be totalled. Because these are three ways of looking at the same thing, the total will be the same in each case.

It is possible to remove some of the simplifying assumptions, to allow for trade, saving, investment, taxation and government spending, and still make these calculations.

Output method

The value of the output of each industry is calculated. To this is added the value of services provided by the public sector, including defence, education and the health service. This information is based on regular censuses of production and on sample data.

Expenditure method

The value of consumer expenditure is calculated. To this is added expenditure by firms on investment goods, expenditure by the government and the difference between exports and imports. Account is also taken of savings. This information is based on regular censuses of distribution and on sample data.

Income method

The total of incomes received by individuals, both as wages and salaries and as profits and dividends, is calculated. To this is added the profits of companies and surpluses made by public corporations. Account is taken of income received from abroad. The main source of all this information is the Board of Inland Revenue.

Problems of calculating the national income

Double counting When using the output method, if the output of all producers is added together there will be some double counting, i.e. some products will be counted more than once. For example, a woollen coat sold in a department store may be considered to be the output of the store, but it also includes the output of the tailor, the weaver, the spinner and the farmer. The solution is either to add in simply the final product at the end of the chain, i.e. the department store's output, or to calculate for each producer the **value added** to products bought in.

Transfer payments When using the income method, if all the income received by individuals is totalled this will include some which does not represent payment for work or other economic activity. For example, student grants, old age pensions and family allowances are different in this respect from wages and dividends. All such transfer payments must be taken off the total of personal incomes.

Unrecorded transactions When a farmer eats his own potatoes, or a painter paints a mechanic's house in return for having his car repaired, it is unlikely that these transactions will appear in any government record, but they are examples of economic activity. In order to take account of this, some allowance is made in output figures. This measurement problem will be more serious for countries which have a high proportion of self-sufficient village communities.

Changes in the value of money One of the main purposes of measuring national income is to be able to make comparisons with past years and with other countries. If the value of the currency in which the measurement is made is itself changing, this will make such comparisons invalid. The only solution is to use index numbers to value one year's figures in terms of an accepted base year.

1 Define the term 'national income'. What difficulties are encountered in measuring the national income? (OX)

Reasons for measuring national income
1 To provide information, by measuring the effectiveness of past policies and by indicating the need for changes in policy, to help the government control the economy.
2 To give some indication about the standard of living of a country in comparison with the same country in previous years and other countries.

Standard of living

It is sometimes said that gross national product per head is the best single indicator of the standard of living of a country. What this figure gives is the share which each person would have if the GNP were to be distributed evenly. This does not happen in any country. The standard of living means the material way in which people live, i.e. it takes account of such things as the food they eat, the clothes they wear, the houses they live in etc. Because different people attach different importance to such things as food and clothing, it follows that individuals may vary in how they rank other people's standards of living. However, as a generalization, it is assumed that a higher income, in real spending terms, represents a higher standard of living. Most governments are committed to improving the standard of living of at least some of the voters and national income figures can be used as some indication of their success. For a full comparison of living standards it would be necessary to take some account of the quality of life and get evidence about health, pollution, overcrowding, hours worked, type of work, and other factors, all of which affect the welfare and happiness of people.

Cost of living

Many students confuse the standard of living with the cost of living. For each individual, his cost of living is the cost of having a particular standard of living. Changes in the cost of living would mean that he has to pay more or less (work more or less) in order to be able to live in the same way. For example, if a car owner, used to driving a given distance each year, is faced with an increase in the price of petrol, then in order to be able to carry on in the same way he will have to pay more and if he does not want to cut down on any other spending, he will have to earn more. People who do not drive cars will not be affected directly by petrol increases, but will be affected to different extents by rises in public transport fares and delivery costs which will contribute to the final cost of other consumer goods. In fact there is no such thing as 'the cost of living' for a country. The nearest thing is an average which gives some indication of the movement of the general price level. For further details see Chapter 12 on 'Inflation'.

2 *Why are national income figures not always a true reflection of the economic welfare of a country?* (JMB) (Amended)
3 *Examine the factors that determine the size of a country's national income.* (JMB)

Growth

Economic growth is often put forward as a solution to many problems. It means that the GNP of a country increases in real terms. To do this it is necessary to use more of one or more of the factors of production either by making fuller use of existing resources, e.g. lowering the school-leaving age to increase the workforce, or by obtaining new resources, e.g. foreign capital. Growth always involves change and this will be unpopular to some sections of the community. National income figures are used to measure the extent of growth being achieved.

Examination preparation

Objective test study material

Prepare definitions for the following

Gross national product   Gross domestic product   Net national
income   Depreciation   Factor cost   Market price   Standard of living
Cost of living   Growth   Transfer payments   Double counting
Calculations Sometimes simple calculations may be set, e.g. deducting
depreciation from GNP to obtain NNI.

Essay questions

What are the major difficulties in calculating the national income?

In this answer in the first paragraph define the national income. Then in
succeeding paragraphs write a separate paragraph on each major problem:
double counting, exports/imports, subsidies/taxation, unpaid services,
transfer payments, nationalized industries, inaccurate returns.

What is the purpose of calculating the national income?

Again in this answer in the first paragraph define the national income.
Then write paragraphs on the reasons for its calculation. The reasons will
include paragraphs on growth of economy measured, comparison with
other years and countries, standard of living, assists government in
carrying out economic policies, etc. You could include a final paragraph
on the problems of comparison.

What factors determine the size of the national income?

The important point in this essay is to realize that any development of
methods of calculation, problems involved in the calculation or the
reasons for calculation will obtain no marks. In many ways the essay is
not a question on the national income but a question on economic growth.

Para 1 Define national income. Perhaps refer to different methods of its
calculation.
Para 2 Mention the availability of natural resources.
Para 3 Discuss the size and efficiency of the labour force.
Para 4 Raise the point about the country's capital equipment along with
the attitude of unions to mechanization.
Para 5 The broad area of government policy should be raised, specifically policies to promote economic growth and policies to slow down
economic growth.

Para 6 The issue of political stability should be discussed.
Para 7 Foreign factors such as the state of world trade and terms of trade should be mentioned.

Possible marking scheme
In each of the first two questions the first paragraph on a definition of national income, perhaps with a reference to measurement, would be worth 4 marks. Every point (problem or reason) would be worth 1 mark with 2 or 3 more potential marks for fuller development.

In the third question para 1 would be worth 2 marks. Para 2 could earn you 1 mark for mentioning it and another for expanding it. Para 3 would be 1 mark for mentioning size, 1 mark for mentioning efficiency and a further 2 marks for expanding this idea. On para 4 both points would be worth 1 mark and a further 2 could be earned for expansion. Mentioning government policies (para 5) could earn you 1 mark and specific encouraging or slowing-down policies another mark each. You could earn 1 mark for mentioning political stability and another for expanding it. For para 7 mentioning foreign factors, the state of world trade and terms of trade could each gain you a mark.

Examination practice

4 *What is economic growth? Why has the UK experienced such a low level of economic growth in recent years?* (ox)

5 *Briefly explain*
   (a) *How is the Gross National Product measured?*
   (b) *Why is it not always a true indication of living standards?* (JMB)

15   International trade

Synopsis The only way in which a relatively small island like Great Britain can support a large population at a high standard of living is by trade. It is important to know the pattern of UK trade and to see the effects, good and bad, international trade can have on the UK economy.

*

International trade is an extension of the principle of the division of labour. When the principle is applied, production increases and the surplus beyond the producer's own needs can be exchanged for other goods/services.

Benefits of international trade

1 A country might lack a number of raw or basic materials essential for a modern industrialized country, e.g Japan needs to import oil, steel, timber etc.
2 A country, for climatic reasons, might be unable to grow economically a wide range of foods, e.g. Britain needs to import coffee, tea, sugar, a wide range of fruits etc.
3 Countries differ in their endowment of natural resources and availability of skilled labour, management experience and efficiently organized subsidiary industries. Because of this, many products can be made more economically in specific countries. If countries specialize in those products in which they have the greatest **relative advantage** and international trade takes place, the best use will be made of world resources. This argument is known as the **theory of comparative costs**. At its simplest level it ignores transport costs and exchange rates, and assumes free movement of goods and services.

4 A number of countries have a limited market because of their small
population, e.g. Switzerland, Luxembourg. To benefit from the
economies of large-scale production, a larger market is essential.
This sometimes applies to even the largest country, e.g. USA
aircraft industry depends on overseas sales for a level of production
which gives full economies of large-scale production.

5 Competition from foreign rivals may spur a domestic industry to
increased efficiency, e.g. British Leyland was reorganized in 1978
partly because of the loss of home car market to foreign
manufacturers.

6 Consumers have a wider range of products from which to choose.
This range of choice is an indication of rising standards of living.

Reasons for restricting international trade

1 To protect **infant industries** (those in an early stage of economic
development). For instance an African country developing its car
industry will be unable to compete, in both costs and efficiency of
finished product, with a major European producer.

2 To allow home industries, which have become less efficient than
foreign competitors, to decline gradually and switch resources to
other production, thus preventing massive, sudden, structural
unemployment, e.g British textiles faced with Asian competition.

3 To protect home industries from unfair foreign competition.
   (a) competitors receiving government aid such as subsidies or tax
       relief.
   (b) competitors selling at less than full cost of production to dispose
       of over-production. This is called **dumping**; it assumes that
       the product cannot be resold in the country of origin.

4 To prevent or improve a situation where there is a balance of
payments deficit.

5 To avoid dependence on other countries for strategical reasons. For
example a nation may restrict imports of food in order to develop a
sound domestic agricultural industry in cases of war.

6 To conform with political policies. For example in recent years the
US restricted trade with China and Cuba.

7 To retaliate to trade restrictions imposed by other countries.

1 What are the advantages of international trade?
Why do countries place restrictions on international trade? (LOND)

Measures used to restrict trade

1 Import duties (**tariffs**) imposed on goods entering the country.

These increase the price of foreign goods on the home market.
2 Import **quotas**. These limit the quantity of imports, e.g. television sets from Eastern Europe.
3 A complete prohibition (**embargo**). This completely stops imports of a specific commodity or all trade with a particular country.
4 Subsidies given to a domestic industry will make the price of home produced goods artificially low and thus make them more competitive. This may substantially reduce the level of imports of that commodity.
5 The government, acting through its central bank, is able to reduce imports by limiting the amount of foreign currency it makes available to those wishing to buy goods from abroad. This is known as **exchange control**.
6 A variety of indirect methods of restricting imports can be adopted. For example
  (a) by insisting on rigorous safety standards a country might be able to reduce imports of foreign cars
  (b) government contracts might be awarded only to domestic firms. The US government often uses this method in purchasing defence equipment.

Pattern of trade

The UK is one of the most important nations in the world. It is only international trade which makes it possible for a relatively small area to support a large population in comparative affluence. The pattern of UK trade may be examined in various ways.

Visibles and invisibles Visibles are goods which are moved from one country to another. Invisibles are services; the most important categories of these for the UK are government expenditure (embassies and overseas military bases), tourism, shipping, insurance, banking and other commercial services.

The main category in UK visible exports is manufactured goods. There has been a significant change in recent years in visible imports: finished manufactures are now the biggest category, not raw materials.

Annual visible exports have exceeded visible imports in value only nine times since 1800.

Export markets In recent years there has been a significant change with 53 per cent of UK exports going to Western Europe in 1978 (37 per cent to the EEC) compared with 31 per cent in 1958. The USA is still the largest single market.

Import supplies Because the UK imports proportionately less food and raw materials, there has been a proportional decline in imports from developing countries (except those producing oil – OPEC countries). The increased production of North Sea oil will drastically affect the pattern of trade in the next few years. Of UK imports 57 per cent came from Western Europe (40 per cent from the EEC) in 1978, compared with 30 per cent in 1958.

Balance of trade
A record of visible imports and visible exports is kept and the difference between them – *plus*, if exports exceed imports, *minus*, if imports exceed exports – is called the **balance of trade**, or sometimes the trade balance. These figures are published monthly in the UK.

Terms of trade
This measures the purchasing power of a country's exports in terms of its imports. If a country needs less exports to pay for the same volume of imports the terms of trade are said to be favourable or to have moved in the country's favour. If more exports are needed to pay for the same volume of imports the terms of trade are adverse or unfavourable. Index numbers are used to make the calculation:

$$\frac{\text{index of average export prices}}{\text{index of average import prices}} \times 100$$

Payment for international trade
Each independent country has its own currency controlled by its own government. Usually a national currency is acceptable only in its country of origin. If international trade takes place, either the seller will insist on payment in his own currency, or he will want to change foreign currency received in payment into his own currency. Either way there will have to be a system for changing money from one currency to another.

Foreign exchange markets Because there is a need for foreign currencies outside their countries of origin, a market exists made up of buyers and sellers. These are specialist foreign exchange dealers and banks and central banks.

Free exchange rates Under this system, sometimes called **flexible exchange rates** or **free convertibility**, the market forces of supply and demand are allowed to determine the relative values of different currencies. The possibility of violent swings makes this unattractive to traders who often work on small margins which can be wiped out by changes in exchange rates.

Fixed exchange rates Countries agree to relate their currencies to a stable value, either the price of **gold** or a **reserve currency**, i.e. one that will be accepted generally for international payments. The central bank of each country has to act against market forces if there is a tendency for the rate to move away from its fixed point. This may lead to unpopular economic policies being applied at home simply to maintain the fixed exchange rate.

Devaluation This is a formal lowering of the fixed exchange rate and results in cheaper exports and dearer imports. Despite its apparent advantages, it is usually regarded as a sign of weakness in the devaluing country.

Revaluation This is the reverse of devaluation and since it makes exports less competitive and imports cheaper, it is unpopular with home producers.

Floating exchange rates In effect this is the same as a free exchange system. It is implied that it is only for a limited period and that when the 'true' market has been established there will be a return to fixed exchange rates. However, the UK has had a floating pound since 1972.

Balance of payments

The balance of payments account for the UK is usually presented with the following categories

1 Current balance
2 Investment and other capital flows
3 Balancing item
4 Balance for official financing
5 Net transactions with the IMF
6 Foreign currency borrowing by the government
7 Changes in official reserves
8 Total official financing

It is important to understand what is meant by each term and to see how they relate to one another. Arithmetically, $1 + 2 + 3 = 4$ and $5 + 6 + 7 = 8$. Also $4 = 8$ (but one is positive and the other negative). Items 1, 2 and 3 summarize the economic activity which has taken place over a year, involving the UK with the rest of the world – items 5, 6 and 7 show how a deficit was paid for or what was done with a surplus. A good analogy can be made to the economic life of a single family over the course of a year. The first half of the balance of payments table corresponds to the account of what the family has done – consumed food and clothing, earned money by regular jobs, had occasional windfalls at bingo, purchased some long lasting items such as a freezer or a house. The second half of the table shows what has happened to the bank balance, whether a new loan has been necessary or whether some of the mortgage has been paid off.

Current balance This is calculated by adding the effects of invisible imports and exports to the trade balance.

Investment and other capital flows This summarizes the effects of such transactions as UK firms building factories in Europe or Japanese firms building factories in Scotland, and loan transactions, short and long term, between UK residents and foreign organizations.

Balancing item Although it can sometimes be very large, this is simply an acceptance of the fact that it is not always possible to keep an accurate track of all transactions: some may not be recorded at all, others may be recorded at different times. The Bank of England can see what is actually happening by changes in the official reserves which it holds.

Net transactions with IMF The International Monetary Fund was set up in 1947 to help member countries with currency problems. It works rather like a bank offering short-term loans to help to keep a business turning over.

Foreign currency borrowing by the government Like businesses using other sources of credit, as well as bank loans, the government, usually through the Bank of England, borrows from, or makes loans to, other central banks or other institutions.

Official reserves The Bank of England holds stocks of gold and foreign currencies for the government.

Balance of payments problems

Although variations from year to year are to be expected, if a country has a persistent adverse balance, i.e. the balance for official financing is usually negative, calling for repeated borrowing, this is taken to be a sign that something is wrong. Again using the personal analogy, it is like a family always spending more than it earns and getting further and further into debt. As in the analogy there are several alternative policies which a government can follow, but they are all unpopular with some sections of the community.

2 *What is meant by 'total currency flow'? What measures can be taken by governments to achieve a satisfactory balance of payments situation?*
(AEB)

Examination preparation

Objective test study material

Prepare definitions for the following

Comparative cost theory   Infant industry   Subsidies   Dumping
Tariffs   Quotas   Embargo   Exchange control   Balance of trade
Balance of payments   Invisible items of trade   Investment and
capital flows   Official financing   Balancing item   Devaluation
Terms of trade

Diagrammatical material

You should be able to calculate a balance of trade surplus or deficit or a
balance of payments surplus or deficit from figures presented. You should
also be able to calculate the effects of a devaluation on import and export
prices and also the terms of trade. Sometimes candidates may be asked to
obtain figures from graphs.

Essay questions

*How can a country reduce the levels of its imports? In what circumstances
might a country be justified in adopting such a policy?*

Para 1 Introduce the essay by saying that measures can be taken to
reduce imports of specific goods or the general level of imports. Note that
in this question you are not required to distinguish between the two.

Paras 2-7 Define and explain tariffs, quotas, embargo, subsidies,
exchange controls and indirect methods.

Para 8 Introduce the second half of the question by pointing out that
the reasons for restriction can be political or simply retaliatory. But here
you are concerned only with economic reasons.

Para 9 Explain the argument about infant industries.

Para 10 Discuss the need to maintain employment in important
industries.

Para 11 Raise the argument about protecting home industries against
unfair competition.

Para 12 Point out the problem of a balance of payments deficit.

Possible marking scheme

Paras 1–7 should be worth 2 marks each up to a maximum of 8 marks
because this is the fairly simple part of the question. Paras 8–12 should
be worth up to 4 marks each up to a maximum of 12 marks.

Examination practice

3 (a) *Discuss the factors that might lead to an increase in the import of cars.*
  (b) *For what reasons might a government place restrictions on such imports?* (LOND)
4 (a) *Define the term 'balance of payments'.*
  (b) *Explain what information is recorded in the balance of payments.* (RSA)

16 The government and the economy

Synopsis The British economy is a mixed economy, an economy where the major economic questions are answered in part by the government, in part by individuals. The government seeks to eradicate the inherent weaknesses of a free enterprise economy, whilst, at the same time, achieving the advantages such a system offers. In the main, therefore, government intervention is associated with the problems of capitalism. However, there is a more positive side to government intervention. The government seeks to promote an economic climate where free enterprise thrives – for example, the government attempts to reduce the level of inflation. There is also a 'welfare' economic reason for government intervention.

*

Summary of government economic policy goals

Policies designed to ensure a balance of payments equilibrium A variety of policies have been pursued by governments intending to reduce imports, increase exports, or possibly both. The policies include tariffs, quotas, prohibitions, devaluation, trade fairs, subsidies to exports, assisting in credit arrangements and so forth. All governments realize that no economy can survive unless it is able to pay its foreign debts.

Policies designed to curb the rate of inflation It is generally accepted that any rate of inflation above 2–3 per cent has damaging economic and social effects. A variety of policies have been adopted to reduce demand and keep costs increasing at as low a rate as possible.

Policies to maintain high levels of employment All governments have accepted responsibility for maintaining full employment and all have adopted policies to achieve this objective.

Regional policy In addition to maintaining a high national rate of employment, governments, in their regional policies, have tried to ensure that particular regions do not suffer unemployment above the national average.

Consumer legislation In a free enterprise system there is the danger of consumer exploitation. The danger has been recognized by successive governments and this has been reflected in a variety of Acts of Parliament seeking to control monopolies, protect the consumer against misleading advertising, paying excessive interest rates for credit, etc.

Welfare economics Governments attempt to ensure that all citizens enjoy a minimum standard of living. The tax system is the major weapon adopted by governments to redistribute the wealth of the country. High income groups pay proportionately more in taxation than do lower income groups. The money thus collected goes back to lower income groups in the way of family income supplements, child benefits, etc.

Economic growth Growth and the direction of that growth is an important field of government activity. Growth depends on investment – the government can help stimulate investment by creating the correct economic climate including low rates of inflation, tax incentives, balance of payments equilibrium. However, it must ensure that the investment is in the right areas for future economic growth – e.g. investment in capital equipment and not office blocks and service industries. This is difficult to achieve in a free society. If persuasion fails, the government is forced to invest directly. In the UK there have been grants and loans to nationalized industries and loans to firms in vital sectors and investment through the National Enterprise Board.

Conditions of work Historically, capitalism was associated with the exploitation of the workforce – long hours, low rates of pay, dangerous conditions. Considerable legislation has been passed by Parliament limiting the number of hours worked, ensuring safe working conditions, through the Wages Councils stating minimum rates of pay, protecting workers against wrongful dismissal, specifying redundancy payments, etc.

Central government grants to local authorities These have permitted local authorities to assume many responsibilities that in other countries are the responsibility of the central government, e.g. education. Therefore over 60 per cent of local expenditure is provided for by central government in the form of grants in order that local democracy can continue to work.

The questions below are typical of those you may face on this part of the syllabus.

1 *Give reasons for the increase in government intervention in the economy since 1945.* (LOND) (Amended)
2 *How can a government attempt to increase investment in the economy?* (AEB)
3 *How does the government attempt to influence the distribution of income in the economy?* (JMB

Glossary

Note *italicized words and phrases* will be found under their own glossary entry.

Ageing population A situation where the average age of the population, recorded over a number of years, is increasing. This may be caused by a falling *birth-rate* or a falling *death-rate*.

Aggregate demand The total planned expenditure on goods and services by consumers, firms and the government in an economy.

Average cost Sometimes called unit cost, it is the cost of producing one unit of output. It is calculated by dividing total costs by output.

Balance of payments The published account of one nation's financial dealings with the rest of the world. The UK figures are presented in three sections: *current account*; capital movements; *official financing*.

Balance of trade A record of all visible exports and imports for one country with the rest of the world. The *current account* of the *balance of payments* is calculated by adding on invisible exports and imports.

Balanced/deficit/surplus budget The budget is the government's revenue-raising statement for the coming financial year. If it intends to spend exactly the amount raised, it is a balanced budget; if intended spending is more than revenue, it is a deficit budget; if intended spending is less than revenue, it is a surplus budget.

Balancing item An item included in the *balance of payments* to take account of transactions not recorded, recorded incorrectly, or recorded outside the accounting period. It is the difference between the actual changes in reserves held by the Bank of England and the recorded changes attributable to transactions.

Birth-rate A measure of the number of children being born in any year in relation to the total size of the population. It is normally expressed as so many live births per thousand of the population.

Capital The factor of production which consists of man-made resources, e.g. factories, machines and roads. To obtain capital, some *investment* must have taken place, i.e. immediate consumption was postponed so that further production could take place.

Capital intensive When applied to a firm or an industry, this means that the proportion of *capital* to *labour* is very high. An extreme case would be a fully automated factory with no labour.

Capitalism An economic system where private ownership of *capital* is permitted. Production decisions are made by firms or individuals and consumers have freedom of choice.

Collectivism A system of organizing the economic life of a community whereby the state owns and controls capital resources and plans and organizes production in the interests of the community. It is sometimes called a planned economy.

Contraction of demand/supply This term is used to describe a reduction in demand/supply, brought about by a change in price. Graphically, it is shown as a movement along the demand/supply curve.

Co-operative In the UK, this type of business organization is usually confined to retailing, but occasionally there may be producer co-operatives. The members of the society own the business and profits are distributed in the form of dividends related to the extent to which the member has made use of or contributed to the co-operative.

Cost of living This is a way of measuring price changes. In reality, every individual's cost of living will depend on the style in which he lives. Index numbers, based on prices for certain standard commodities, are used to give an indication of the general movement in prices. The most important measure is the retail prices index.

Cost-push inflation A rise in the general price level which is caused by increased costs of raw materials, power and labour being passed on to the consumers in higher prices for goods and services.

Creeping inflation A gradual rise in the price level over a period of years.

Current account The part of the *balance of payments* that records visible and invisible exports and imports.

Cyclical unemployment Unemployment which is caused by in-adequate demand for labour associated with the slumps of the trade cycle.

Death-rate A measure of the number of people dying in any year in relation to the total size of the population. It is usually expressed as so many deaths per thousand of the population.

Debentures Loans to a company which are usually secured to some particular asset. Debenture holders receive a fixed rate of interest but they are not shareholders.

Declining population A situation where the population of a country over a period of years is falling. It may be due to a falling *birth-rate* or a rising *death-rate* or to an increase in *net migration*.

Demand-pull inflation A rise in the general price level which is caused by an increase in purchasing power (wages) greater than the increase in production.

Dependent population Those people in the total population who are not part of the workforce. It includes children below school-leaving age and retired people.

Depreciation The allowance that has to be made for the value of capital used up over time. In national income accounting, it is the difference between *gross national product* and net national product.

Derived demand A situation where the demand for one thing depends on the demand for something else, e.g. the demand for coalminers depends on the demand for coal.

Devaluation A lowering of a fixed exchange rate of one currency in relation to others.

Direct/indirect taxation Direct taxes are levied directly on individuals, e.g. income tax and capital transfer tax. They can be graduated according to ability to pay. Indirect taxes are taxes on expenditure, e.g. VAT, customs and excise duties.

Diversification The opposite of specialization; it can describe a region where there is a wide variety of industries and also apply to multi-product firms.

Division of labour This principle depends on the advantages which come from specialization. Work is shared out amongst the total number of workers so that each man is responsible for a part of the job and all are dependent on each other for the end product.

Double counting This is a possible cause of error in national income accounting where the output of one industry may include the output of another industry, e.g. paper production and books. The solution is either to use the value added at each stage or to count only final products.

Dumping When one country sells its products in another country at very low prices, either to try to capture a market or to dispose of over-production without lowering the home price.

Economic rent Extra income received by any *factor of production* because of a shortage of supply, e.g. city centre sites and 'pop' singers.

Economies/diseconomies of scale Economies are reductions in the *average cost* of production which occur as total output is increased up to a point; diseconomies are the increases in average costs which occur when total output is increased beyond the optimum (lowest average cost) level.

Elasticity of demand/supply Price elasticity of demand/supply is a measure of how the demand/supply of an item will respond to changes in the price of that item. This is the most common use of elasticity, but it is also possible to talk about income elasticity of demand/supply, that is to say when the effects of income changes are measured; and also cross elasticity, when the effects of price changes in other items are measured.

Embargo A method of restricting trade by which the import or export of certain goods is forbidden or all trade with certain countries is forbidden.

Enterprise The *factor of production* which consists of that type of *labour* which organizes production. Entrepreneurs bring together the other factors of production and bear the risk of success or failure. In most developed economies it is not possible to make a clear distinction between enterprise and labour.

Equilibrium price The price at which the quantity demanded by buyers equals the quantity offered for sale by suppliers.

Exchange controls Limitations placed by the government of a country on its citizens restricting the amount of gold and foreign currency they may hold. It is usually an attempt to control trade or deal with *balance of payments* problems.

Extension of demand/supply This term is used to describe an increase in demand/supply brought about by a change in price. Graphically it is shown as a movement along the demand/supply curve.

External economies/diseconomies Any reduction/increase in costs of production which result from factors outside the control of an individual firm but which arise because of the location of the firm, e.g. transport facilities.

Factor cost In national income accounting, goods and services are valued in terms of the resources used to produce them in contrast to *market price* valuation which is what consumers pay. The difference between factor cost and market price is made up of taxes and *subsidies*.

Factors of production/factor resources A way of classifying the economic resources of a community which can be used to produce goods and services. The human factors are *labour* and *enterprise*, the non-human factors are *land* and *capital*.

Fiscal policy A general term for the way in which the government uses *public expenditure* and the raising of tax revenue to control the economy.

Fixed costs Those costs incurred in production that do not vary with output, e.g. rent, rates, interest charges. The spreading of fixed costs over increasing output is one cause of *economies of scale*.

Footloose When applied to an industry, this term means that there are no strong advantages to locating it in one region rather than any other region.

Frictional unemployment *Unemployment* which arises from the imperfect working of the economic system. It is caused by temporary immobility of *labour* as workers who have lost jobs cannot immediately find suitable new jobs.

Full employment An economic policy goal for most modern governments. It can be defined in several ways, e.g. 'unemployment is not beyond an acceptable level' or 'the number of unfilled vacancies is greater than the number registered unemployed'.

Galloping inflation A situation when the general price level is rising so fast that the public loses confidence in money.

Geographical mobility The extent to which *labour* can change jobs by moving from one part of the country to another. Immobility is one of the causes of *unemployment*.

Gross domestic product (GDP) The value of the final output, goods and services, produced within an economy.

Gross national product (GNP) The total output of goods and services produced by a country in a given year. In contrast to GDP all overseas earnings, including property income, are included. Neither GDP nor GNP take account of *depreciation*.

Gross wages Earnings before compulsory deductions for tax and national insurance are made.

Growth This is an increase in productive capacity, usually expressed as changes in the national income over a period of time, measured in constant terms.

Horizontal integration The joining together of two or more firms engaged in the same sphere of activity. This may take place by merger or take-over. The most likely reasons for this are either to gain *economies of scale* or to reduce competition.

Income redistribution Sometimes a policy goal for governments, the usual aim is to use *progressive* taxation, such as income tax and capital taxes, to take from the rich and provide special benefits for the low paid.

Infant industry An industry in the early stages of development which is thought to need protection from foreign competitors. This protection is usually in the form of *tariff* barriers or *subsidies*.

Inferior good Anything which is considered to be a cheap substitute for a more attractive good or service, e.g. public transport and private cars; take-aways and West End restaurants. As real income rises, consumers buy less of the inferior good and transfer to the better alternative.

Inflation An increase in the general price level in an economy (see *cost-push inflation* and *demand-pull inflation*).

Investment The creation of *capital*.

Investment and other capital flows The way in which the *balance of payments* account records all financial transactions which are not identifiable as visible or *invisible* current items. It includes short and long-term loans and investment by foreign firms in the UK and by UK firms abroad.

Invisibles (items of trade) Payment for services given or received by foreigners. The main items are government expenditure, tourism, shipping, insurance and banking.

Joint stock company A firm with a number of 'owners' – shareholders who each have *limited liability*. Private joint stock companies have from two to fifty shareholders and shares are not freely transferable. Public joint stock companies have a minimum of seven shareholders and shares are usually freely transferable through the Stock Exchange.

Labour The *factor of production* which consists of human resources, originally clearly distinguishable from *enterprise* but now usually considered with it as the available workforce of a community.

Labour intensive When applied to a firm or an industry, this means that the proportion of *labour* to *capital* is very high. An extreme case would be the way that slave labour was used to build the Pyramids.

Land The *factor of production* which consists of natural resources, including the earth, the sea, rivers, lakes, vegetation and minerals.

Limited liability A legal limitation on the extent to which a shareholder or partner can be held responsible for the debts of a firm. He cannot be called upon to meet more than the paid-up value of his shares or an agreed amount in a partnership (note that at least one partner must have unlimited liability).

Marginal cost The change in total costs when output is increased or decreased by one unit.

Market forces Supply and demand acting freely to determine the *equilibrium price* of goods and services.

Market price   A term used in national income accounting (see *factor cost*).

Mixed economy   An economic system where the state owns some capital and undertakes some planning of production and control of economic activity, but there is also a large amount of private enterprise.

Monetary policy   Actions and intentions of the government to control the money supply. The aims of monetary policy are to control *inflation* and deflation.

Money wages   The amount of wages paid measured in terms of the current value of money. By contrast, *real wages* measure the purchasing power of wages by taking into account price changes.

Net migration   The number of emigrants from a country subtracted from the number of immigrants coming to a country. This, together with births and deaths, determines the size of the population.

Net national income   That amount of the *GNP* which is available for consumption and new *investment*, after allowance has been made for replacing and maintaining existing *capital*.

Net wages   *Gross wages* less compulsory deductions.

Occupational mobility   The extent to which *labour* can change jobs from one occupation to another. Application of the *division of labour* often reduces occupational mobility.

Official financing   The section of the *balance of payments* account which records government borrowing or repayment of loans from abroad, and changes in official reserves of gold and foreign currencies.

Opportunity cost   The *real cost* of using economic resources for one purpose is the value of the alternative uses to which they could have been put.

Optimum population   The level of population in a country at which *GNP* per head is maximized.

Overpopulation   A situation where increases in the population lead to a decrease in *GNP* per head.

Percentage tax   Tax is levied at a fixed rate and the burden of tax on the payer is proportional and not *progressive*, e.g. standard rate of income tax.

Piece rate   A method of wage payment by which earnings are related directly to output – workers are paid so much per unit produced.

Poverty trap   A situation where an increase in *money wages* may result in a fall in real income. It is usually associated with social benefits, e.g. free school meals, which depend on income levels.

Primary production The extraction of basic or raw materials by industries such as farming, forestry, fishing, mining and quarrying.

Private company See *joint stock company*.

Private sector That part of the economy which consists of businesses owned and controlled by private citizens. It includes sole proprietors, partnerships and *joint stock companies*.

Productivity A measure of the output of any one factor. It is usually used in reference to labour productivity. Increased labour productivity can normally be achieved only by increasing inputs of other factors, e.g. *capital*.

Progressive/regressive taxation Progressive taxation is taxation where the burden of tax becomes proportionately heavier with increased ability to pay, e.g. higher rates of personal tax. Regressive taxation either places heavier burdens on those with smaller incomes or, more usually, places the same burden on everyone, thereby in fact hitting the low paid hardest. All indirect taxes are regressive in this way.

Public company A *joint stock company* with at least seven shareholders. The annual accounts are published and shares may be bought by members of the public.

Public corporation One of the ways in which a nationalized industry may be organized. Day-to-day administration is left to a chairman and board, but Parliament appoints these people and decides on major policy.

Public expenditure Spending by central and local government and nationalized industries.

Public sector That part of the economy which is owned and controlled by the state. It includes the nationalized industries and government departments (Ministries).

Public sector borrowing requirement (PSBR) This is the annual sum required by nationalized industries, other government bodies, e.g. the Health Service, and local authorities, for capital expenditure which cannot be met out of current income.

Pull and push measures Describes methods used by governments to influence the location of industry. Pull measures are incentives (the carrot); push measures are penalties (the stick).

Quotas A way of restricting trade by limiting the import of certain commodities to a fixed number.

Real cost See *opportunity cost*.

Real wages See *money wages*.

Redundancy A situation where labour is no longer needed. It may occur because there is no demand for the product, as with a declining industry, or because the method of production changes from *labour intensive* to *capital intensive*.

Residual unemployment *Unemployment* which cannot be explained by any other reason. It usually refers to workers who are unfit to take on the responsibility of a full-time job.

Seasonal unemployment When the demand for *labour*, in certain industries, is seasonal, e.g. hotels, it follows that at other times this labour will be unemployed unless a corresponding job can be found for the rest of the year.

Secondary production The manufacture of goods and building and construction industries.

Shares Claims to part of the profits of a *joint stock company*, titles to part ownership of the company.

Shifts in demand/supply This term is used to describe changes in demand/supply brought about for reasons other than price changes. Graphically it is shown by redrawing the demand/supply curve.

Social costs/social benefits The disadvantages/advantages accruing to a community as a by-product of a firm, e.g. pollution or improved communications.

Standard of living A measure of the material way in which life is lived.

Structural unemployment *Unemployment* which is caused by the decline of an industry.

Subsidies Negative taxes. Producers are given money by the government to reduce effective costs.

Tariffs Import duties placed on goods entering a country; the result is to make imported goods dearer and therefore less competitive with home-produced goods.

Technological unemployment *Unemployment* caused by mechanization or any other reason which leads to more *capital intensive* industry.

Terms of trade The comparative values of a country's imports and exports. It is measured as the index of export prices over the index of import prices.

Tertiary production The provision of services, either as part of the production chain bringing primary and secondary products to the consumer, or satisfying a direct need of the consumer, or carrying out administrative work.

Time rate A method of wage payment by which workers are paid an agreed amount, by the day, week, or month, regardless of output.

Transfer payment A term used in national income accounting to describe income which is received when no economic activity has taken place, e.g. student grants.

Underpopulation A situation in which an increase in the population would lead to an increase in *GNP* per head. It usually means that a country's resources are not being fully used.

Unemployment Usually reserved for *labour*, this term refers to that part of the workforce which is available for work but is unable to find it.

Utility A good or service possesses utility if it is capable of satisfying a *want*.

Variable costs Those costs which change as output changes, e.g. raw materials.

Vertical integration The expansion of a business by merger or take-over, either backwards to gain control of supplies or forwards to gain control of markets.

Wage drift A term which refers to the gap which appears in certain circumstances between basic wage rates and earnings. It happens when *labour* is in short supply and employers bid against each other to compete for available labour.

Wants Anything which will satisfy a human need and requires economic resources to obtain it.

Weight-gaining/weight-losing industries Weight-gaining means that the end product of an industry is bulkier than its component parts, e.g. cars. Weight-losing means that the end product is lighter or less bulky than its raw materials, e.g. steel.

Working population The total number of people in a country offering themselves for work (also known as the labour force). It includes all those registered as unemployed.

Index

Entries indexed *G* will be found in the Glossary, p.142.

Also available

John Daintith
A Dictionary of Physical Sciences £2.95

Stella E. Stiegeler
A Dictionary of Earth Sciences £2.95

E. A. Martin
A Dictionary of Life Sciences £2.95

Anthony Flew
A Dictionary of Philosophy £3.95

Roger Scruton
A Dictionary of Political Thought £3.95

Russell Langlev
Practical Statistics £1.95

This book provides a simple description of the principle and practical application of statistics which will appeal both to the non-mathematician and to those who are more involved in the subject. It will be especially useful to students of such subjects as Physical, Life and Earth Sciences, Psychology, Medicine and Business Studies, who need a concise and straightforward introduction to the use of statistical method.

Robert Seton Lawrence
A Guide to Speaking in Public £1.75

Here is a wealth of sound and practical advice, presented with examples both of great oratory and of the many pitfalls which the careful speaker can learn to avoid. This guide – highly recommended by many managerial and professional organizations – includes sections on how to: gain confidence; secure and hold an audience's attention: get people to enjoy listening to you; think logically; project your personality; cope with speaking at formal occasions; plus: developing children; the art of conversation; common speech faults and their cure; public speaking examinations.

Reference, language and information

☐	**A Guide to Insurance**	Margaret Allen	£1.95p
☐	**The Story of Language**	C. L. Barber	£1.95p
☐	**North-South**	Brandt Commission	£2.50p
☐	**Test Your IQ**	Butler and Pirie	£1.25p
☐	**Writing English**	D. J. Collinson	£1.50p
☐	**Manifesto**	Francis Cripps et al.	£1.95p
☐	**Illustrating Computers**	Colin Day and Donald Alcock	£1.95p
☐	**Buying and Selling a House or Flat**	Marjorie Giles	£1.75p
☐	**Save It! The Energy Consumer's Handbook**	Hammond, Newport and Russell	£1.25p
☐	**Mathematics for the Million**	L. Hogben	£1.95p
☐	**Dictionary of Famous Quotations**	Robin Hyman	£2.95p
☐	**Militant Islam**	Godfrey Jansen	£1.50p
☐	**The War Atlas**	Michael Kidron and Dan Smith	£5.95p
☐	**Practical Statistics**	R. Langley	£1.95p
☐	**How to Study**	H. Maddox	£1.95p
☐	**The Limits to Growth**	D. H. Meadows et al.	£2.50p
☐	**Your Guide to the Law**	ed. Michael Molyneux	£3.95p
☐	**Ogilvy on Advertising**	David Ogilvy	£6.95p
☐	**Common Security**	Palme Commission	£1.95p
☐	**The Modern Crossword Dictionary**	Norman Pulsford	£2.95p
☐	**A Guide to Saving and Investment**	James Rowlatt	£2.50p
☐	**Career Choice**	Audrey Segal	£2.95p
☐	**Logic and its Limits**	Patrick Shaw	£2.95p
☐	**Names for Boys and Girls**	L. Sleigh and C. Johnson	£1.95p
☐	**Straight and Crooked Thinking**	R. H. Thouless	£1.95p
☐	**First Clue: The A-Z of Finding Out**	Robert Walker	£2.50p
☐	**Money Matters**	Harriet Wilson	£1.25p
☐	**Dictionary of Earth Sciences**		£2.95p
☐	**Dictionary of Economics and Commerce**		£1.50p
☐	**Dictionary of Life Sciences**		£2.95p
☐	**Dictionary of Physical Sciences**		£2.95p
☐	**Harrap's New Pocket French and English Dictionary**		£2.50p

☐ **Pan Dictionary of Synonyms and Antonyms**		£1.95p
☐ **Travellers' Multilingual Phrasebook**		£1.95p
☐ **Universal Encyclopaedia of Mathematics**		£2.95p

Literature guides

☐ **An Introduction to Shakespeare and his Contemporaries**	Marguerite Alexander	£2.95p
☐ **An Introduction to Fifty American Poets**	Peter Jones	£1.75p
☐ **An Introduction to Fifty Modern British Plays**	Benedict Nightingale	£2.95p
☐ **An Introduction to Fifty American Novels**	Ian Ousby	£1.95p
☐ **An Introduction to Fifty British Novels 1600–1900**	Gilbert Phelps	£2.50p
☐ **An Introduction to Fifty Modern European Poets**	John Pilling	£2.95p
☐ **An Introduction to Fifty British Poets 1300–1900**	Michael Schmidt	£1.95p
☐ **An Introduction to Fifty Modern British Poets**		£2.95p
☐ **An Introduction to Fifty European Novels**	Martin Seymour-Smith	£1.95p
☐ **An Introduction to Fifty British Plays 1660–1900**	John Cargill Thompson	£1.95p

All these books are available at your local bookshop or newsagent or can be ordered direct from the publisher. Indicate the number of copies required and fill in the form below   11

....

Name_____
(Block letters please)

Address_____

_____

Send to CS Department, Pan Books Ltd, PO Box 40, Basingstoke, Hants
Please enclose remittance to the value of the cover price plus:
35p for the first book plus 15p per copy for each additional book ordered
to a maximum charge of £1.25 to cover postage and packing
Applicable only in the UK

While every effort is made to keep prices low, it is sometimes
necessary to increase prices at short notice. Pan Books reserve
the right to show on covers and charge new retail prices which
may differ from those advertised in the text or elsewhere